# BLUE WAVE
## FISHING SUP

An Accounting Practice Set with GS˙
Using Perpetual Inventory Records,
a One-Month Accounting Cycle

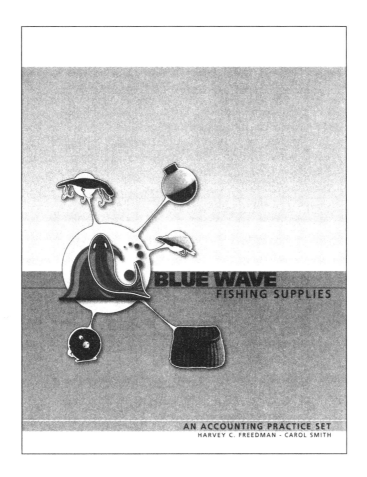

HARVEY C. FREEDMAN, C.G.A.
HUMBER INSTITUTE OF TECHNOLOGY
& ADVANCED LEARNING

CAROL SMITH, C.M.A.
HUMBER INSTITUTE OF TECHNOLOGY
& ADVANCED LEARNING

THOMSON

NELSON

Australia   Canada   Mexico   Singapore   Spain   United Kingdom   United States

**Blue Wave Fishing Supplies: An Accounting Practice Set**

by Harvey C. Freedman and Carol Smith

**Associate Vice President, Editorial Director:**
Evelyn Veitch

**Publisher:**
Rod Banister

**Senior Marketing Manager:**
Charmaine Sherlock

**Developmental Editor:**
Natalie Barrington

**Permissions Coordinator:**
Kristiina Bowering

**Senior Production Editor:**
Julie van Veen

**Proofreader:**
Edie Franks

**Production Coordinator:**
Cathy Deak

**Design Director:**
Ken Phipps

**Cover Design:**
Glenn Toddun

**Cover Images:**
Fishing lures: © 2006 Jupiter Images and its Licensors. All rights reserved
Float: Melissa King / Shutterstock
Fishing reel: Angela Hill / Shutterstock
Fishing basket: C Squared Studio / Photodisc Green / Getty Images

**Compositor:**
Diane Van Ingen

**Printer:**
Webcom

**Library and Archives Canada Cataloguing in Publication**

Freedman, Harvey C.

Blue Wave Fishing Supplies : an accounting practice set : with GST, using perpetual inventory records, covering a one-month accounting cycle / Harvey Freedman, Carol Smith.

ISBN 0-17-610463-1

1. Accounting—Problems, exercises, etc. I. Smith, Carol (Carol C.) II. Title.

HF5661.F74 2006    657'.044'076
C2006-900716-0

## Dedication

To all students:

> For continuing to strive for the best that they can be.
> For continuing to ask questions.

To my family:

> Their understanding, encouragement, and support meant a great deal to the completion of this project.

## Acknowledgements

To my students:

> For encouragement for the project and the many ways they came up with new means of looking at the same information.

To my colleagues:

> For continued support and acknowledgement of student success.

To Carol Smith:

> Professor at Humber College, my colleague who was the technical reviewer for this practice set, including solutions, and who provided helpful criticisms.

To Legoria Simmons:

> Educational Assistant at Humber College, my colleague who assisted in checking the manuscript, including solutions, and who provided helpful suggestions.

---

**Tell me and I forget**
**Show me and I remember**
**Let me do it and I understand**

*—Zen proverb*

---

# Contents

# Introduction

**This Practice Set:**

- Was developed to assist the student in understanding the accounting process regarding journals and subledgers.
- **Is not long or complex**.
- Tries to get you to visualize yourself in the role of bookkeeper/accountant.
- Uses **source documents** requiring analysis for proper recording.
- After completing the project, there are general business questions which require you to make decisions about the business.
- Should take between 8 and 12 hours to complete.
- Shows an Income Statement with year-to-date information for the six months ending June 30, 2012 (Jan 1, 2012 to June 30, 2012), and other financial statements.
- Can be completed manually, and/or by using computer data files for use with Simply Accounting by Sage software. The data files can be found at www.freedman.nelson.com. An example of the software Income Statement format is presented in Appendix A on page 61. If you are using computer software to complete the project, your instructor will advise you of the Simply Accounting by Sage software data filename for use with the software available at your school.
- The transactions can be completed using the General Journal with Special Journals and with perpetual inventory, or can use only the General Journal to record transactions.

The objective of this accounting practice set is to provide you with an overall understanding of how accounting information is recorded in journals and transferred between journals, ledgers and sub-ledgers, and inventory records, and then used in financial statement preparation to help managers in making decisions for the future.

This practice set requires you to analyse transactions and make decisions using real lifestyle source documents to issue cheques; record transactions in the appropriate journals; post general ledger, subsidiary, and inventory ledgers; prepare a trial balance and worksheet; record adjusting entries; and prepare financial statements.

The practice set follows real life accounting because the practice set does not close books monthly and allows you to accumulate accounting information to prepare financial statements on a year-to-date activity basis. All financial information is accumulated until the fiscal year-end when the books are closed.

## Suggested Time Schedule for This Practice Set

You can start any time after merchandise inventory with cost of goods sold and/or special journals with a general journal of a first semester accounting course.

For those students who complete a bank reconciliation as part of their course, a blank reconciliation form is provided in Appendix B on page 62 and a bank statement is provided in Appendix C on page 63.

**Taxes**

Goods and Services Tax (GST), Harmonized Tax (HST), Registration for GST, and Provincial Sales Tax, are discussed in Appendix D (Taxes) on page 64.

## Company Background

The business "Blue Wave Fishing Supplies" has been operating for 2-½ years in North Bay, Ontario, and is busy during all fishing seasons, especially during the summer months. The business sells various fishing equipment and supplies to large and small outdoor recreational businesses in the area.

The business is operated from a store with ample parking and has approximately 4,000 square feet of store and warehouse space. The owner Adeline Vogelgesang has two and one-half years left in the 5-year lease. The business pays for hydro, water, business taxes, etc. The store was originally renovated with new shelving and display cases and a working area for showing customers how to use fishing rods and reels, fishing nets, and the best way to store their gear in the various tackle boxes.

The current fiscal year started on January 1, 2012, and the fiscal year-end will be December 31, 2012.

Mrs. Vogelgesang arranged a bank loan on January 2, 2012 with the North Bay Bank for $12,000, with $400 monthly payments due at the end of each month. The $400 payment includes interest. The bank was able to lend Mrs. Vogelgesang the money because she has been a client of the bank since she opened, has paid off her previous business loans, and has been able to provide business financial statements showing the profitability of the business.

As a business student at Cannadore College, you were hired on a part-time basis to record the business transactions and assist with other duties in the store. You will be paid at the end of each month.

You will be replacing the bookkeeping service that has kept the accounting records up to June 30, 2012.

## Description of Blue Wave Fishing Supplies Information

The firm uses the following accounting records.

1. **Files**    Copies of the original source documents are provided with each transaction, including memos received by you from Mrs. Vogelgesang.

2. **Journals**    Note: *SP* refers to Special Journal.  Record transactions in date order.

> **Journals provided:**
> a) *SP* Sales journal              (SJ) records all sales on credit.
> b) *SP* Cash Receipt journal        (CR) records all cash received.
> c) *SP* Purchase journal            (PJ) records all purchases on credit.
> d) *SP* Cash Disbursements journal  (CD) records all cash payments.
> e)    General journal              (GJ) all other transactions not recorded above.

3. **Ledgers**    General and subsidiary

      a) General ledger — this is the main ledger. Separate accounts are kept for each asset, liability, equity, revenue and expense account. The accounts are numbered the same as the Trial Balance.

      b) Subledgers — the totals of the subledger accounts must balance with the total of the control accounts.
            1) Accounts receivable, customers.
            2) Accounts payable, suppliers — sometimes called vendors.

      c) Perpetual Inventory Subledger — the totals of the Perpetual Inventory subledger accounts must balance with the total of the Merchandise Inventory control account.

4. **Other accounting policies or principles**

Capital assets are amortized on a straight line basis.

The revised CICA handbook, section 3060, has recommended the use of the term *amortization* instead of *depreciation*, but the use of the term *depreciation* has not been ruled out. This practice set reflects the recommendations of section 3060. See memo on page 8 of this practice set.

Supplies are debited to the asset when purchased.

Inventory is recorded using the Weighted Average method. Refer to Appendix E for information on this method.

Sales to **wholesale customers**, businesses that sell to other businesses or individuals, are sold with terms of 2/10, n30. NOTE: By law, Provincial Sales tax (PST) or Retail Sales Tax (RST) is not charged to customers that sell products to other businesses or individuals. A business receives a PST exemption number, which requires the seller to not collect PST. The PST Exempt # is on applicable invoices.

Sales to **retail customers**, businesses or individuals that purchase for their own use, are subject to a **8% provincial sales tax (PST).** Cash discounts apply only to customers who buy on credit. Credit cards are not accepted.

Credit sale invoices are in numerical order.

You have arranged credit terms of 2/10, n30 with many of your suppliers for purchases of merchandise, supplies and other services. Other terms are as indicated.

Sales and Purchase discounts for early payment (2/10), applies to the value of merchandise sold or purchased, and supplies and services and does not apply to PST and GST. Sales and Purchase discounts are allowed 1 or 2 days of grace for mail delivery to accommodate weekends or holidays.

Discounts on merchandise purchases should be allocated (normally charged) to the Merchandise Inventory account. In this practice set discounts are recorded in the Purchase Discount account. Discounts are shown separately to indicate that the discounts are part of the Cost of Goods Sold.

Two accounts are used to record GST.

**GST on Sales**, to record GST on sales of merchandise.
**GST on Purchases and Services** (abbreviated Purc/Serv) to record GST on purchases of merchandise for resale, supplies and services; i.e., repair invoices, hydro expense, etc.

The bank loan schedule, on page 12, calculates the interest cost portion of each payment and the remaining principal balance of the loan.

Cheques are issued in numerical order.

The bookkeeping service has brought all of the accounting records up to date, including adjusting entries, as of June 30, 2012 and will be available on a consultation basis if needed.

Expenses have been divided into two categories, sales expenses and office expenses.

Sales have been divided into four broad categories:
Rods & Reels
Tackle Boxes
Fish Nets
Other

The bookkeeping service advised you to record your sales in these categories to assist you in finding out which groups of merchandise are selling better than others.

You will notice that sales items are listed on invoices in a random order, and should be summarized when recording the manual entries (e.g., Tackle Boxes (Best and Better) should be added together and recorded as a one-line entry (Tackle Boxes) in the journal entry).

The accounts are numbered using the following structure:
100's Assets
200's Liabilities
300's Equities
400's Sales and related accounts
51-'s Cost of goods sold and related accounts
52-'s and 53-'s Sales expenses
57-'s Office/Other expenses

The gaps in account numbers such as 401 and 403 are to allow future accounts to be added without breaking the sequence of the account section(s).

The special journals were created with multiple columns for sales to allow you to record data for analysis. The Special Journals (Perpetual Inventory) have columns for Cost of Goods Sold and Merchandise Inventory. The Invoice number column in the Cash Receipts and Cash Disbursements journals is for cross reference purposes (audit trail).

The ending inventory value of goods not sold is checked on a regular basis by Mrs. Vogelgesang and verified by you.

## Ratios

The bookkeeping service and Mrs. Vogelgesang calculated the following ratios (two decimal places) as at June 30.

| | |
|---|---|
| Current Ratio | 6.42 : 1 |
| Acid Test Ratio | 4.88 : 1 |
| | |
| Gross Profit Ratio | 49.52 % |
| Expense Ratio | 31.54 % |
| Net Profit Ratio | 17.99 % |
| | |
| Merchandise Turnover | 12.32 times |
| | |
| Return on Equity | 2.72 % |
| Debt Ratio | 0.338: to 1 |

---

**Current Ratio**

$$\frac{\text{Current Assets}}{\text{Current Liabilities}} =$$

**Acid Test ratio**

$$\frac{\text{Quick Assets}}{\text{Current Liabilities}} =$$

**Gross Profit ratio**

$$\frac{\text{Gross Profit from Sales}}{\text{Net Sales}} =$$

**Expense ratio**

$$\frac{\text{Operating Expenses}}{\text{Net Sales}} =$$

**Net Profit ratio**

$$\frac{\text{Net Profit}}{\text{Net Sales}} =$$

**Merchandise Turnover**

$$\frac{\text{Cost of Goods Sold}}{\text{Average Cost of Inventory}} =$$

**Return on Equity**

$$\frac{\text{Net Income (Profit)}}{\text{Beginning Owner's Equity}} =$$

**Debt Ratio**

$$\frac{\text{Total Liabilities}}{\text{Total Assets}} =$$

The following additional information is available to you.

## Blue Wave Fishing Supplies
### Adjusted Trial Balance
### as of June 30, 2012

| Account Code # | Account Name | Account Balances Debit | Credit |
|---|---|---|---|
| 101 | Bank Account Chequing | 15,625 | |
| 120 | Accounts Receivable | 3,210 | |
| 122 | Merchandise Inventory | 5,150 | |
| 124 | Store Supplies on Hand | 378 | |
| 128 | Prepaid Insurance | 400 | |
| 161 | Store Equipment | 31,500 | |
| 162 | Accum Amortiz Store Equip | | 15,000 |
| 210 | Accounts Payable | | 3,103 |
| 220 | Business Taxes Payable | | -0- |
| 241 | GST on Sales | | 1,501 |
| 243 | GST on Purc/Serv | 786 | |
| 248 | PST Payable | | 40 |
| 261 | Bank Loan Payable | | 10,072 |
| 310 | Capital    A. Vogelgesang | | 8,325 |
| 315 | Drawings A. Vogelgesang | 3,600 | |
| 401 | Sales – Rod & Reel | | 59,256 |
| 403 | Sales – Tackle Boxes | | 43,200 |
| 405 | Sales – Nets | | 19,780 |
| 407 | Sales – Other | | 6,400 |
| 421 | Sales – Returns | 830 | |
| 423 | Sales – Discounts | 2,124 | |
| 510 | Cost of Goods Sold | 64,634 | |
| 516 | Purchase – Discounts | | 1,195 |
| 521 | Rent Expense | 12,000 | |
| 523 | Store Salaries Expense | 12,650 | |
| 525 | Security Expense | 600 | |
| 527 | Store Supplies Expense | 941 | |
| 529 | Insurance Expense | 1,200 | |
| 531 | Hydro and Water Expense | 512 | |
| 533 | Amortization Expense Equip | 3,000 | |
| 535 | Advertising Expense | 6,680 | |
| 537 | Business Taxes Expense | 720 | |
| 572 | Miscellaneous Expense | 260 | |
| 574 | Bank Charges/Interest Expense | 472 | |
| 576 | Bookkeeping Expense | 600 | |
| | Totals | $167,872 | $167,872 |

The Accounts Receivable and Accounts Payable subsidiary customers and vendors are:

**Schedule of Accounts Receivable**
**At June 30, 2012**

| # | Customer Name | Invoice # | Invoice Date | Sale Amount | GST Amount | Invoice Amount |
|---|---|---|---|---|---|---|
| C1 | Central Lake RV Centre | 680 | June 01, 2012 | $1,000 | $ 70 | $1,070 |
| C2 | North River Lodge | 703 | June 28, 2012 | $900 | $63 | 963 |
| C3 | Trout Lake Resort | 698 | June 22, 2012 | $1,100 | $77 | 1,177 |
| | | | | | Total | $3,210 |

**Schedule of Accounts Payable**
**At June 30, 2012**

| # | Supplier Name | Invoice # | Invoice Date | Purchase Amount | GST Amount | Invoice Amount |
|---|---|---|---|---|---|---|
| S1 | Fishing Accessories Inc. | 685 | June 29, 2012 | $900 | $63 | $ 963 |
| S2 | Rods & Reels Company | 2987 | June 29, 2012 | $1,300 | $91 | 1,391 |
| S3 | Laredo Tackle Boxes Ltd. | 832 | June 29, 2012 | $700 | $49 | 749 |
| | | | | | Total | $3,103 |

**Schedule of Merchandise Inventory Items**
**At June 30, 2012**

| Item Code | Item Description | Items in Stock | Item Average Cost | Value In stock @ Average Cost | Normal Selling Price |
|---|---|---|---|---|---|
| CL-Lg | Coolers- Large | 6 | 20.0000 | 120.00 | $40 |
| CL-Md | Coolers- Medium | 3 | 15.0000 | 45.00 | $30 |
| FH-1 | Assorted Fish Hooks | 140 | 5.0000 | 700.00 | $10 |
| FL-1 | Fishing Line | 33 | 10.0000 | 330.00 | $20 |
| Net-Bes | Net- Best | 14 | 35.0000 | 490.00 | $70 |
| Net-Bet | Net- Better | 10 | 25.0000 | 250.00 | $50 |
| Rod-1 | Rod Reel set 1 | 12 | 45.0000 | 540.00 | $90 |
| Rod-2 | Rod Reel set 2 | 15 | 55.0000 | 825.00 | $110 |
| Rod-3 | Rod Reel set 3 | 12 | 70.0000 | 840.00 | $140 |
| TK-Bes | Tackle Boxes- Best | 16 | 35.0000 | 560.00 | $70 |
| TK-Bet | Tackle Boxes- Better | 18 | 25.0000 | 450.00 | $50 |
| | Total Inventory at Cost | | | 5,150.00 | |

The account balances and inventory items and values above have been entered in the general ledger and subledgers provided.

**Blue Wave Fishing Supplies**

2637 Highway 18 East, North Bay, Ontario P1B 7G8

Date:     June 30, 2012  ( Copy of Original Memo )

To:       Adeline Vogelgesang, Owner

From:     Sarah Davis, Accounting Service

---

From information supplied by you.

Total value of Store Equipment purchased is per Store Equipment General Ledger Account #161. All equipment was purchased on January 2, 2010.

Normal life expectancy for this type of equipment is 5 years.

Estimated trade-in allowance is approximately $ 1,500.00.

Based on the above, we have adjusted the amortization on a monthly basis to June 30. We would suggest you make a monthly entry to adjust amortization.

I have photocopied this memo, to remind you to process a monthly transaction.

*Sarah Davis*

## Blue Wave Fishing Supplies
### Worksheet
### for 6 months ending June 30, 2012

| | ACCOUNT TITLES | Trial Balance Debit | Trial Balance Credit | Adjustments Debit | Adjustments Credit | Adjusted Trial Balance Debit | Adjusted Trial Balance Credit | Income Statement Debit | Income Statement Credit | Balance Sheet Debit | Balance Sheet Credit |
|---|---|---|---|---|---|---|---|---|---|---|---|
| 101 | Bank Account Chequing | 15,625 | | | | 15,625 | | | | 15,625 | |
| 120 | Accounts Receivable | 3,210 | | | | 3,210 | | | | 3,210 | |
| 122 | Merchandise Inventory | 5150 | | | | 5,150 | | | | 5,150 | |
| 124 | Store Supplies on Hand | 433 | | | a 55 | 378 | | | | 378 | |
| 128 | Prepaid Insurance | 600 | | | b 200 | 400 | | | | 400 | |
| 161 | Store Equipment | 31,500 | | | | 31,500 | | | | 31,500 | |
| 162 | Accum Amortiz Store Equip | | 14,500 | | c 500 | | 15,000 | | | | 15,000 |
| 210 | Accounts Payable | | 3,103 | | | | 3,103 | | | | 3,103 |
| 220 | Business Taxes Payable | | 0 | | | | 0 | | | | 0 |
| 241 | GST on Sales | | 1,501 | | | | 1,501 | | | | 1,501 |
| 243 | GST on Purc/Serv | 786 | | | | 786 | | | | 786 | |
| 248 | PST Payable | | 40 | | | | 40 | | | | 40 |
| 261 | Bank Loan Payable | | 10,072 | | | | 10,072 | | | | 10,072 |
| 310 | Capital A. Vogelgesang | | 8,325 | | | | 8,325 | | | | 8,325 |
| 315 | Drawings A. Vogelgesang | 3,600 | | | | 3,600 | | | | 3,600 | |
| 401 | Sales - Rod & Reel sets | | 59,256 | | | | 59,256 | | 59,256 | | |
| 403 | Sales - Tackle Boxes | | 43,200 | | | | 43,200 | | 43,200 | | |
| 405 | Sales - Nets | | 19,780 | | | | 19,780 | | 19,780 | | |
| 407 | Sales - Other | | 6,400 | | | | 6,400 | | 6,400 | | |
| 421 | Sales - Returns | 830 | | | | 830 | | 830 | | | |
| 423 | Sales - Discounts | 2,124 | | | | 2,124 | | 2,124 | | | |
| 510 | Cost of Goods Sold | 64,634 | | | | 64,634 | | 64,634 | | | |
| 516 | Purchase - Discounts | | 1,195 | | | | 1,195 | | 1,195 | | |
| 521 | Rent Expense | 12,000 | | | | 12,000 | | 12,000 | | | |
| 523 | Store Salaries Expense | 12,650 | | | | 12,650 | | 12,650 | | | |
| 525 | Security Expense | 600 | | | | 600 | | 600 | | | |
| 527 | Store Supplies Expense | 886 | | a 55 | | 941 | | 941 | | | |
| 529 | Insurance Expense | 1,000 | | b 200 | | 1,200 | | 1,200 | | | |
| 531 | Hydro and Water Expense | 512 | | | | 512 | | 512 | | | |
| 533 | Amortization Expense Equip | 2,500 | | c 500 | | 3,000 | | 3,000 | | | |
| 535 | Advertising Expense | 6,680 | | | | 6,680 | | 6,680 | | | |
| 537 | Business Taxes Expense | 720 | | | | 720 | | 720 | | | |
| 572 | Miscellaneous Expense | 260 | | | | 260 | | 260 | | | |
| 574 | Bank Charges/Interest Expense | 472 | | | | 472 | | 472 | | | |
| 576 | Bookkeeping Expense | 600 | | | | 600 | | 600 | | | |
| | | 167,372 | 167,372 | 755 | 755 | 167,872 | 167,872 | 107,223 | 129,831 | 60,649 | 38,041 |
| | Net Income for period | | | | | | | 22,608 | | | 22,608 |
| | | | | | | | | 129,831 | 129,831 | 60,649 | 60,649 |

**An Accounting Practice Set**

## Blue Wave Fishing Supplies
## Income Statement
## for the 6 months ended June 30, 2012

**Revenue from Sales**

| | | | |
|---|---|---|---|
| Sales - Rod & Reel sets | | $ 59,256 | |
| Sales - Tackle Boxes | | 43,200 | |
| Sales - Nets | | 19,780 | |
| Sales - Other | | 6,400 | |
| Total Sales | | | $128,636 |
| Less: Sales - Returns | | $ 830 | |
| Sales - Discounts | | 2,124 | |
| Sales Deductions - Total | | | 2,954 |
| Net Sales | | | $125,682 | 100% |

**Cost of Goods Sold**

| | | | | |
|---|---|---|---|---|
| Cost of Goods Sold | | 64,634 | | |
| Less: Purchase - Discounts | | 1,195 | | |
| Net Cost of Goods Sold | | | $63,439 | 50.5% |
| Gross Profit on Sales | | | $62,243 | 49.5% |

**Operating Expenses**

**Sales Expenses**

| | | | | |
|---|---|---|---|---|
| Rent Expense | $ 12,000 | | | |
| Store Salaries Expense | 12,650 | | | |
| Security Expenses | 600 | | | |
| Store Supplies Expense | 941 | | | |
| Insurance Expense | 1,200 | | | |
| Hydro and Water Expense | 512 | | | |
| Amortization Expense | 3,000 | | | |
| Advertising Expense | 6,680 | | | |
| Business Taxes Expense | 720 | | | |
| Total Sales Expenses | | 38,303 | | |

**General Expenses**

| | | | | |
|---|---|---|---|---|
| Miscellaneous Expense | 260 | | | |
| Bank Charges/Interest Expense | 472 | | | |
| Bookkeeping Expense | 600 | | | |
| Total General Expenses | | 1,239 | | |
| Total Operating Expenses | | | 39,635 | 31.5% |
| Net Income (Profit) | | | $22,608 | 18.0% |

## Blue Wave Fishing Supplies
### Statement of Changes in Owner's Equity
### for the 6 months ended June 30, 2012

| | | |
|---|---:|---:|
| Capital January 1, 2012 | | $ 8,325 |
| Add: Investments by Owner | $ -0- | |
| Net Income from statement | 22,608 | 22,608 |
| Subtotal | | 30,933 |
| Less: Drawings | | 3,600 |
| Capital June 30, 2012 | | $ 27,333 |

## Blue Wave Fishing Supplies
### Balance Sheet
### June 30, 2012

#### ASSETS

**Current Assets**

| | | |
|---|---:|---:|
| Bank Account Chequing | $ 15,625 | |
| Accounts Receivable | 3,210 | |
| Merchandise Inventory | 5,150 | |
| Store Supplies on Hand | 378 | |
| Prepaid Insurance | 400 | |
| Total Current Assets | | $24,763 |

**Capital Assets**

| | | |
|---|---:|---:|
| Store Equipment | 31,500 | |
| Less: Accum Amortization | 15,000 | |
| Total Capital Assets | | 16,500 |
| Total Assets | | $ 41,263 |

**Current Liabilities**

| | | |
|---|---:|---:|
| Accounts Payable | | 3,103 |
| Business Taxes Payable | | -0- |
| GST Charged on Sales | 1,501 | |
| Less: GST Paid on Purc/Serv | 786 | |
| Net GST Payable | | 715 |
| Provincial Sales Tax Payable | | 40 |
| Total Current Liabilities | | 3,858 |

**Long-Term Liabilities**

| | | |
|---|---:|---:|
| Bank Loan Payable | | 10,072 |
| Total Liabilities | | 13,930 |

**OWNER'S EQUITY**

| | | |
|---|---:|---:|
| Capital A. Vogelgesang | | 27,333 |
| Total Liability and Equities | | $ 41,263 |

# Bank Loan Schedule

NOTE: This schedule should be used when making the loan payment entry on page 28.

North Bay Bank
309 Massey Drive
North Bay, Ontario
P1A 9B6

Issued    Jan 2, 2012

Interest Rate   0.0850%

Loan To:    **Blue Wave Fishing Supplies**
2637 Highway 18 East
North Bay, Ontario
P1B 7G8

**** Note:   All amounts have been rounded to nearest dollar
for ease in completing project

| Date Payment Made | Period | Payment Required | Days | Interest Rate 0.0850% Interest | Reduction To Loan | Loan Balance Remaining |
|---|---|---|---|---|---|---|
| Jan 02 | | | | | | 12,000 |
| Jan 31 | 1 | 400 | 30 | 84 | 316 | 11,684 |
| Feb 29 | 2 | 400 | 29 | 79 | 321 | 11,363 |
| Mar 31 | 3 | 400 | 31 | 82 | 318 | 11,045 |
| Apr 30 | 4 | 400 | 30 | 77 | 323 | 10,722 |
| May 31 | 5 | 400 | 31 | 77 | 323 | 10,399 |
| Jun 30 | 6 | 400 | 30 | 73 | 327 | 10,072 |
| Jul 31 | 7 | 400 | 31 | 73 | 327 | 9,745 |
| Aug 31 | 8 | 400 | 31 | 70 | 330 | 9,415 |
| Sep 30 | 9 | 400 | 30 | 66 | 334 | 9,081 |
| Oct 31 | 10 | 400 | 31 | 66 | 334 | 8,747 |
| Nov 30 | 11 | 400 | 30 | 61 | 339 | 8,408 |
| Dec 31 | 12 | 400 | 31 | 61 | 339 | 8,069 |
| | | 4,800 | | 869 | 3,931 | |

## Requirements

The ending balances for the general ledger, subledgers, and perpetual inventory items as of June 30, have been entered.

The transactions in source document form, for July 2012 are presented on page 16.

Unless otherwise directed by your instructor, you should complete the practice set in the following order.

1.   **Journalize** — Analyze the document for each transaction and record each (**Journalize**) in the appropriate journal as discussed earlier.

   You will issue cheques and add provincial sales tax to customer invoices if the PST (Provincial Sales Tax) exempt number is not shown.

   When the firm purchases merchandise for resale to other customers, the merchandise is purchased provincial sales tax (PST) exempt. This means the business does not pay provincial sales tax (PST) on the items purchased. You will compare customer records to cheques received to decide if cash discounts are applicable. You will decide if cash discounts are to be taken when paying your suppliers.

2.   a) If you are using **special journals with group total posting** and one general journal, follow these instructions.

   **Posting** — Based on the entries that you made in the journals, post to the ledger accounts and subsidiary accounts as follows:

   i) Daily posting — post the **individual amounts** from the accounts receivable and accounts payable columns to the accounts receivable and accounts payable subledgers. If inventory items are being purchased or sold, post the number of items and the average cost (the average cost may need to be recalculated if the purchase price is higher than the previous average cost). Refer to Appendix E on page 65: for information on calculating the Average Cost of Inventory.

   ii) Daily postings — post any amount in the other column(s) to the general ledger accounts.

   iii) End of month — total all journals to ensure they are in balance. Debits equal credits.

   iv) End of month — post the applicable special journal totals to the general ledger accounts.

   When posting, cross reference the journal page number and the ledger account number, respectively, in the posting reference column (PR) of the ledger and special journals. Use Customer (C) and Supplier (S) numbers as shown in the subledgers to indicate posting to the subledger.

If you are using perpetual inventory records, cross reference the journal page number and the inventory code number, respectively, in the posting reference column (PR) of the ledger and inventory records.

A checkmark ✓ should be used in the Journal column **Inven Post Ref** to indicate posting to the Inventory subledger.

b) If you are using **general journals with individual postings** for each transaction, post each transaction to the general ledger and when required to the accounts receivable, accounts payable and inventory subledgers (refer to Appendix E page 65).

When posting, cross reference the journal page number and the ledger account number, respectively, in the posting reference column (PR) of the ledger and general journals. Use Customer (C) and Supplier (S) numbers as shown in the subledgers to indicate posting to the subledger.

3. a) Trial Balance:
   Prepare a July 30, 2012, trial balance before calculating any adjusting entries. This trial balance can be prepared on the blank worksheet provided on page 53. You may also prepare the trial balance and complete the worksheet using the Excel worksheet provided on the www.freedman.nelson.com website with the file name: WsJuly-Perpetual.xls.

   Continue with adjusting entries only when the trial balance has equal total debit and credit amounts.

   b) Complete the worksheet adjustment columns by using the data supplied by memos on July 31. Complete the worksheet by extending each amount to the income statement and balance sheet columns.

4. Prepare schedules of accounts receivable, accounts payable and inventory, on the forms provided. Balance these amounts to the general ledger control accounts.

5. Financial Statements — prepare the following statements on the forms provided.

   a) Income statement for the period January 1 to July 31 with cost of goods section. The **year-to-date** amounts are from the general ledger.

   b) Statement of Changes in Owner's Equity for period January 1 to July 31.

   c) Balance Sheet, as at close of business, July 31.

6. Journalize the adjusting entries from the worksheet in the general journal, and post to the general ledger.

7. Your instructor may require you to prepare a trial balance after the adjusting entries have been posted to ensure the accuracy of your data.

8.    Calculate the ratios on page 58 . Compare them to the ratios at June 30.

      Current Ratio
      Acid Test Ratio
      Gross Profit Ratio
      Expense Ratio
      Net Profit Ratio
      Merchandise Turnover
      Return on Equity
      Debt Ratio

9.    After all the reports have been prepared, analyze the information to answer the additional
      questions on page 59. Your instructor may assign additional questions.

# Transactions (source documents received or given during July)

**Jul 2**    Issued cheque 612 to Central Mall Management for $2,000 plus 7% GST as per lease agreement.

| No. 612 | $_____ | | |
|---|---|---|---|
| Date _____ 20___ | | | |
| To _____ | | | |
| For _____ | | | |
| Balance Forward | 15,625.00 | | |
| Deposited | | | |
| Deposited | | | |
| Deposited | | | |
| Subtotal | | | |
| This Cheque | | | |
| Balance | | | |

**Blue Wave Fishing Supplies**
2637 Highway 18 East
North Bay, Ontario P1B 7G8

612

Date _____
DD MM YYYY

PAY TO THE
ORDER OF _____ $_____

_____/100 DOLLARS

North Bay Bank
309 Massey Drive
North Bay, Ontario
P1A 9B6

Blue Wave Fishing Supplies

_____

⑆612⑆ ⑈213488721⑈ ⑉0411⑉

---

**Jul 2**    Ordered and received from Fishing Accessories Inc.

**Fishing Accessories Inc.**
120 Hampshire Way
Milton, Ontario L9T 2Y5

Date: ___Jul 2, 2012___
Invoice #: ___691___
Terms: ___2/10, n30___

Sold to:  Blue Wave Fishing Supplies
2637 Highway 18 East
North Bay, Ontario
P1B 7G8

Ship to:
Same

| Quantity | Description | Price | Total |
|---|---|---|---|
| 12 | Coolers - Medium | 15.00 | 180.00 |
| 16 | Coolers - Large | 20.00 | 320.00 |
| | Total before taxes | | 500.00 |
| PST Exempt # 89-63B | Provincial Sales Tax @ 8% | | Exempt |
| Our GST # B-17866 | GST @ 7% | | 35.00 |
| | Invoice Total | | $ 535.00 |

**Jul 3**  Trout Lake Resort returned from original invoice #698, 4 Tackle boxes– Better, because the latch work (the part that locks the top and bottom together) is defective.

**INVOICE 698Rt**

## Blue Wave Fishing Supplies
2637 Highway 18 East, North Bay, Ontario P1B 7G8

Date: ___Jul 3, 2012___
Terms: ___Original Inv #698___

Sold to:  Trout Lake Resort
1285 Brunel Road
Trout Lake, Ontario
P1H 9R6

| Quantity | Description | Price | Total |
|---|---|---|---|
| -4 | Tackle Boxes - Better<br>Defective latch | 50.00 | (200.00) |
| | Total before taxes | | (200.00) |

PST Exempt # 93X-B45   Provincial Sales Tax (8%)
GST #GS-4368        GST @ 7%

THIS IS A CREDIT NOTE        $ _____

DO NOT PAY

**Jul 3**  Returned the 4 Tackle boxes– Better to Fishing Accessories Inc. for credit from original invoice 685.

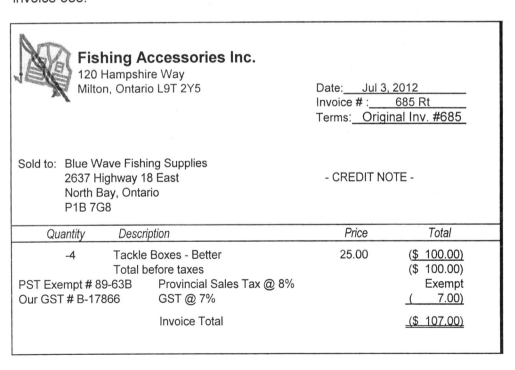

## Fishing Accessories Inc.
120 Hampshire Way
Milton, Ontario L9T 2Y5

Date:___Jul 3, 2012___
Invoice # : ___685 Rt___
Terms:___Original Inv. #685___

Sold to:  Blue Wave Fishing Supplies
2637 Highway 18 East
North Bay, Ontario
P1B 7G8

- CREDIT NOTE -

| Quantity | Description | Price | Total |
|---|---|---|---|
| -4 | Tackle Boxes - Better | 25.00 | ($ 100.00) |
| | Total before taxes | | ($ 100.00) |
| PST Exempt # 89-63B | Provincial Sales Tax @ 8% | | Exempt |
| Our GST # B-17866 | GST @ 7% | | ( 7.00) |
| | Invoice Total | | ($ 107.00) |

**Jul 4**   Issue cheque to pay invoice #433.

---

**Invoice # 433**

## Canadian Security Services
1260 Lawson Street, North Bay, Ontario P1B 2M9
Phone : (123) 887-4004     Fax : (123) 887-4010

Date: _____July 4, 2012_____     Terms:____2/10, n30_____
                                       Customer Contact: ___JJ_____

Sold to : Blue Wave Fishing Supplies
          2637 Highway 18 East
          North Bay, ON
          P1B 7G8

| | **Total Charges** |
|---|---|

| | | |
|---|---|---|
| Security service for the month of July 2012 | | $ 100.00 |
| | Subtotal | 100.00 |
| | PST: | nil |
| Our GST # is X-2569 | GST @ 7% | 7.00 |
| | Please Pay | $ 107.00 |

---

| No. 613   $_____ | | **Blue Wave Fishing Supplies** | 613 |
|---|---|---|---|
| Date _____ 20___ | | 2637 Highway 18 East |  |
| To _____ | | North Bay, Ontario P1B 7G8 | |
| For _____ | | Date _____ |
| | | | DD MM YYYY |

| Balance Forward | |
|---|---|
| Deposited | |
| Deposited | |
| Deposited | |
| Subtotal | |
| This Cheque | |
| Balance | |

PAY TO THE
ORDER OF _____ $_____

_____ /100 DOLLARS

North Bay Bank                    Blue Wave Fishing Supplies
309 Massey Drive
North Bay, Ontario
P1A 9B6                           _____

⑆613⑆ ⑈213488 71⑈ ⑆041 1⑆

---

**Jul 5**   Sold the following to Outdoor Outfitters on invoice #712.

**INVOICE 712**

## Blue Wave Fishing Supplies
2637 Highway 18 East, North Bay, Ontario P1B 7G8

Date: ___Jul 5, 2012___
Terms: ___2/10, n30___

Sold to:  Outdoor Outfitters Inc.
135 Ash Street
Callander, ON
P0H 7P6

| Quantity | Description | Price | Total |
|---|---|---|---|
| 10 | Tackle Boxes - Better | 50.00 | $   500.00 |
| 6 | Tackle Boxes - Best | 70.00 | 420.00 |
| 7 | Coolers - Large | 40.00 | 280.00 |
| 5 | Rod & Reel set - 3 | 140.00 | 700.00 |
|  | Total before taxes |  | $ 1,900.00 |

PST Exempt #93X-B458   Provincial Sales Tax @ 8%
Our GST #GS-4368    GST  @ 7%    _____

Invoice Total    $ _____

**Jul 6**   Bought store supplies from Supplies & More (a new vendor/supplier). Note: All bags will be stamped with the company logo and address, therefore they are not returnable.

### Supplies & More
*1263 Metcalfe Street, North Bay, Ontario P1B 8N4*
*GST #: GSP831*

Date: ___Jul 6, 2012___    Invoice #: ___6685___
Terms: ___2/10, net 30___

Sold to : Blue Wave Fishing Supplies    Ship to:
2637 Highway 18 East     Same
North Bay, Ontario P1B 7G8

| Qty. | Items | | Cost | Total |
|---|---|---|---|---|
| 1 | Box | Price Tags | 15.00 | 15.00 |
| 10 | Boxes | Bags Medium | 8.50 | 85.00 |
| 10 | Boxes | Bags Large | 10.00 | 100.00 |
|  |  | Total before taxes | | $ 200.00 |
|  |  | Provincial Sales Tax @ 8% | | 16.00 |
|  |  | GST @ 7% | | 14.00 |
|  |  | Invoice Total | | $ 230.00 |

*Note:*
Cost of Store Supplies for business is $216.00 (includes PST).

**Jul 6**    Sale to North River Lodge, invoice #713, 2/10, net 30.

---

**INVOICE 713**

## Blue Wave Fishing Supplies
2637 Highway 18 East, North Bay, Ontario P1B 7G8

Date:    <u>Jul 6, 2012</u>
Terms:    <u>2/10, n30</u>

Sold to:   North River Lodge
           212 Riverside Drive
           Thorne, ON
           P0H 9A8

| Quantity | Description | Price | Total |
|---|---|---|---|
| 5 | Rod & Reel set - 2 | 110.00 | $ 550.00 |
| 1 | Net - Better | 50.00 | 50.00 |
| 10 | Net - Best | 70.00 | 700.00 |
| | Total before taxes | | $ 1,300.00 |

PST Exempt #AC-78-25H    Provincial Sales Tax @ 8%
Our GST #GS-4368         GST @ 7%        _____

                                 Invoice Total        $ _____

---

**Jul 9**    Payment to Rods & Reels Company for invoice #2987.

---

No. 614      $_____

Date _____ 20___

To _____

For _____

| Balance Forward | |
|---|---|
| Deposited | |
| Deposited | |
| Deposited | |
| Subtotal | |
| This Cheque | |
| Balance | |

## Blue Wave Fishing Supplies      614
2637 Highway 18 East
North Bay, Ontario P1B 7G8

Date _____
            DD MM YYYY

PAY TO THE
ORDER OF _____ $_____

_____ /100 DOLLARS

North Bay Bank             Blue Wave Fishing Supplies
309 Massey Drive
North Bay, Ontario
P1A 9B6             _____

⑈614⑈ ⑆213488 71⑈ ⑈0411⑈

---

                                                         **Blue Wave Fishing Supplies**

**Jul 10**   Purchase from Laredo Tackle Boxes Ltd. with new inventory item.

**Laredo Tackle Boxes Ltd.**
635 Main Street
Mississauga, Ontario
L5M 3P7

Date:   July 10, 2012

INVOICE # **855**

Sold to : Blue Wave Fishing Supplies
             2637 Highway 18 East
             North Bay, Ontario
             P1B 7G8

Ship to:
Same

| Date Ordered | Terms | P.O. No. | Ship via |
|---|---|---|---|
| July 10, 2012 | 2/10, n30 | | |

| Qty. | Description | Price each | Total | |
|---|---|---|---|---|
| 40 | Folding Chairs | 10.75 | $   430.00 | new item |
| 19 | Tackle Boxes - Better | 26.00 | 494.00 | higher cost |
| 16 | Tackle Boxes - Best | 36.00 | 576.00 | higher cost |

PST Exempt # 89-63B
Our GST # FS-3840

| | |
|---|---|
| Total before taxes | 1,500.00 |
| Shipping | Included |
| Prov Sales Tax @ 8% | Exempt |
| GST @ 7% | 105.00 |
| Invoice Total | $  1,605.00 |

> If you are using Simply
> software, use:
> Inventory Code: FC-01
> Inventory Description: Folding
> Chairs
> Selling Price: $20.00
> Minimum quantity: 5

**Jul 11**   Sale to Trout Lake Resort.

INVOICE  714

**Blue Wave Fishing Supplies**
2637 Highway 18 East, North Bay, Ontario P1B 7G8

Date:   Jul 11, 2012
Terms:   2/10, n30

Sold to:   Trout Lake Resort
               1285 Brunel Rd
               Trout Lake, Ontario
               P1H 9R6

| Quantity | Description | Price | Total |
|---|---|---|---|
| 4 | Tackle Boxes - Best | 70.00 | $   280.00 |
| 3 | Rod & Reel set -2 | 110.00 | 330.00 |
| 5 | Folding Chairs | 20.00 | 100.00 |
| 4 | Fishing Line | 20.00 | 80.00 |
| 3 | Net - Best | 70.00 | 210.00 |

PST Exempt #93X-B45
Our GST #GS-4368

| | |
|---|---|
| Total before taxes | $ 1,000.00 |
| Provincial Sales Tax @ 8% | |
| GST  @ 7% | |
| Invoice Total | $ |

**Jul 18**  Mrs. Vogelgesang gave you this memo.

### Blue Wave Fishing Supplies
2637 Highway 18 East, North Bay, Ontario P1B 7G8

**Memo**

Date:  July 18, 2012  ( Copy of Original Memo )

To:  Student's Name _____

From:  Adeline Vogelgesang, Owner

Please pay invoice #12-842 from Harland's Heating & Air Conditioning for $642.00 (amount includes GST) to pay for repairs to my home air conditioning unit. The repairs were completed yesterday.

*Adeline*

| No. 615        $_____ | | |
|---|---|---|
| Date _____ 20___ | | |
| To _____ | | |
| For _____ | | |
| Balance Forward | | |
| Deposited | | |
| Deposited | | |
| Deposited | | |
| Subtotal | | |
| This Cheque | | |
| Balance | | |

### Blue Wave Fishing Supplies
2637 Highway 18 East
North Bay, Ontario P1B 7G8

615

Date _____
DD MM YYYY

PAY TO THE
ORDER OF _____ $_____

_____/100 DOLLARS

North Bay Bank
309 Massey Drive
North Bay, Ontario
P1A 9B6

Blue Wave Fishing Supplies

_____

⑆615⑈ ⑆21348871⑈ ⑆0411⑈

**Jul 20**  Received cheque #943 as partial payment for invoice #680.

### Central Lake RV Centre
2561 Jane Street
North Bay, Ontario P0H 9A8
Phone (123) 889-7171

943

20 07 2012
DD MM YYYY

To the
Order Of ____ Blue Wave Fishing Supplies ____ $ 500.00

PAY  Five Hundred ----------------------------------------------------------00/100  DOLLARS

Bank of Ontario
5689 3rd Avenue
North Bay, ON P0H 1A1

**Central Lake RV Centre**

*T L Lake*

_____

⑆943⑈ ⑆2677⑈17⑈ 414⑈

**Jul 20**   Received cheque #1076 as payment for invoices #698 and #714.

```
Trout Lake Resort                                          1076
1285 Brunel Road
Trout Lake, Ontario P1H 9R6          Date:    20 07 2012
Phone (123) 889-7171                         DD MM YYYY


To the
Order Of    Blue Wave Fishing Supplies              $ 2,013.00

PAY  Two thousand thirteen and-----------------------------------------00/100 DOLLARS

        Bank of the North                      Trout Lake Resort
        221294 South Street
        North Bay, Ontario P0H 1A1             Robert Wilson

    ⑈1076⑈    ⑈339967 7⑈ 12⑈     8 28⑈
```

**Jul 23**   Retail sale to friend of family (record a friend's name). Received cheque #103, for invoice #715.

```
                                              INVOICE  715

        Blue Wave Fishing Supplies
        2637 Highway 18 East, North Bay, Ontario P1B 7G8
                            Date:    Jul 23, 2012
                            Terms:   Cash

Sold to: _____ A Friend's Name
         Address
         Town, Province
         Postal Code
```

| Quantity | Description | Price | Total |
|---|---|---|---|
| 1 | Cooler- Large (slightly damaged) | 30.00 | $   30.00 |
| 7 | Assorted Fish Hooks | 10.00 | 70.00 |
| | Total before taxes | | $ 100.00 |
| | Provincial Sales Tax @ 8% | | |
| Our GST #GS-4368 | GST @ 7% | | _____ |
| | Invoice Total | | $ _____ |

```
_____ A Friend's Name     Bank of Nova Scotia        103
                             816 First Avenue
  Address, Town, Your Province   Town, Your Province Postal Code
  Postal Code
                                DATE   23 07 2012
                                       DD MM YYYY
To The
Order of      Blue Wave Fishing Supplies

  PAY  One hundred fifteen -------------------------00/100 DOLLARS $ 115.00


                                     A Friend's Name

    ⑈103⑈ ⑈11300 1⑈  91   9906⑈
```

**Jul 24** Issued cheque to pay for advertising flyers being delivered in today's business mailing. Note: There is no PST on advertising flyers.

| INVOICE | | | | | 876 |
|---|---|---|---|---|---|

Advertising Plus
106 Talon Street
North Bay, Ontario
P1A 7B9

Date __Jul 24, 2012__

_Blue Wave Fishing Supplies_
_2637 Highway 18 East_
_North Bay, Ontario, P1B 7G8_

| SOLD BY | SHIP TO Same | CHARGE COD | ON ACCT. | ACCT FWD -O- | |
|---|---|---|---|---|---|
| 800 Coloured flyers @.75/ea | | | 600 | 00 | |
| | | Subtotal | 600 | 00 | |
| | | PST | Exempt | | |
| Our GST #R-5883 | | GST 7% | 42 | 00 | |
| | | Total | 642 | 00 | |
| | | | | | |
| Terms: COD | | | | | |
| | | | | | |
| Refund needs this receipt. | | | | | |

No. 616    $_____

Date _____ 20__

To _____

For _____

| Balance Forward | |
|---|---|
| Deposited | |
| Deposited | |
| Deposited | |
| Subtotal | |
| This Cheque | |
| Balance | |
| | |

**Blue Wave Fishing Supplies**          616
2637 Highway 18 East
North Bay, Ontario P1B 7G8

Date _____
                    DD MM YYYY

PAY TO THE
ORDER OF _____ $_____

_____/100 DOLLARS

North Bay Bank                Blue Wave Fishing Supplies
309 Massey Drive
North Bay, Ontario
P1A 9B6                        _____

⑊616⑊ ⑊213488 7⑊ ⑊041⑊

**Blue Wave Fishing Supplies**

**Jul 30**  Sale to new customer. The manager is checking on future credit terms for this customer.  Received a $450.00 partial payment.

**INVOICE 716**

# Blue Wave Fishing Supplies
2637 Highway 18 East, North Bay, Ontario P1B 7G8

Date: __Jul 30, 2012__
Terms: __Net 15 days__

Sold to:  Noble's Teen Camp
7893 Trout Lake Road
North Bay, Ontario
P1B 3T4

| Quantity | Description | Price | Total |
|---|---|---|---|
| 10 | Folding Chairs | 20.00 | $   200.00 |
| 4 | Rod & Reel set - 2 | 110.00 | 440.00 |
| 3 | Tackle Box - Better | 50.00 | 150.00 |
| 3 | Tackle Box - Best | 70.00 | 210.00 |
|  | Total before taxes |  | $ 1,000.00 |
|  | Provincial Sales Tax @ 8% |  |  |
|  | GST @ 7% |  | _____ |
|  | Invoice Total |  | $ _____ |

Our GST #GS-4368

Author's suggestion:
Record this transaction as
2 transactions.
1. A credit sale
2. Receipt of the $450.00

---

**Noble's Teen Camp**                                                         **498**
7893 Trout Lake Road
North Bay, Ontario P1B 3T4
Phone (123) 442-TEEN

DATE: __30 07 2012__
DD MM YYYY

PAY  Four hundred fifty and -----------------------------------------------00/100-Dollars     $450.00

To The
Order       Blue Wave Fishing Supplies
2637 Highway 18 East
North Bay, Ontario, P1B 7G8

Noble's Teen Camp

*Irving Noble*

Town Credit Union
5896 Main Street
North Bay, Ont.  P1B 1A1

⑈498⑈  ⑈016622⑈02⑈  ⑈11028⑈

**Jul 31**  Issued Purchase order #66. Tackle boxes are to be delivered tomorrow (August 1).

---

PURCHASE ORDER  #66

# Blue Wave Fishing Supplies
2637 Highway 18 East, North Bay, Ontario P1B 7G8

Date: _Jul 31, 2012_
Delivery date: _Aug 01, 2012_
Terms: _2/10, n30_

To:  Laredo Tackle Boxes Ltd.
635 Main Street
Mississauga, Ontario
L5M 3P7

| Quantity | Items | Unit Price | Total |
|---|---|---|---|
| 15 | Tackle Boxes - Best | 35.00 | $   525.00 |
| 11 | Tackle Boxes - Better | 25.00 | 275.00 |
|  | Total before taxes |  | $   800.00 |

PST Exempt #89-63B    Provincial Sales Tax @ 8%
Our GST #GS-4368     GST  @ 7%    _____

Total PO    $_____

---

**Jul 31**  Issue cheque to pay you $1,040.00 for July work. Split amount to Store Salaries Expense $940.00 and Bookkeeping Expense $100.00. (Ignore CPP, EI and Income Tax.)

---

No. 617    $_____
Date _____ 20___
To _____
For _____

| Balance Forward | |
|---|---|
| Deposited | |
| Deposited | |
| Deposited | |
| Subtotal | |
| This Cheque | |
| Balance | |
| | |

# Blue Wave Fishing Supplies
2637 Highway 18 East
North Bay, Ontario P1B 7G8

617

Date _____
DD MM YYYY

PAY TO THE
ORDER OF _____ $_____

_____/100 DOLLARS

North Bay Bank          Blue Wave Fishing Supplies
309 Massey Drive
North Bay, Ontario
P1A 9B6                  _____

⑆617⑈ ⑉213488 71⑈ ⑈0411⑈

**Jul 31**  Issue cheque to pay Receiver General for June GST balances.

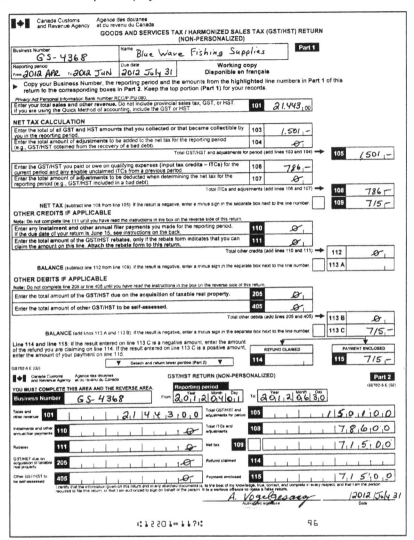

*Canada Revenue Agency. Reproduced with permission of the Minister of Public Works and Government Services Canada, 2006.*

| No. 618 | $ | |
|---|---|---|
| Date | 20 | |
| To | | |
| For | | |
| Balance Forward | | |
| Deposited | | |
| Deposited | | |
| Deposited | | |
| Subtotal | | |
| This Cheque | | |
| Balance | | |

**Blue Wave Fishing Supplies**  618
2637 Highway 18 East
North Bay, Ontario P1B 7G8

Date _____
DD MM YYYY

PAY TO THE
ORDER OF _____ $_____

_____ /100 DOLLARS

North Bay Bank            Blue Wave Fishing Supplies
309 Massey Drive
North Bay, Ontario
P1A 9B6

⑆618⑆ ⑈21348871⑈ ⑉011⑉

**Jul 31**   Received the following bank debit memo.

---

### North Bay Bank

**DEBIT**

309 Massey Drive, North Bay, Ontario P1A 9B6

Date: _July 31, 2012_

From: _____ Blue Wave Fishing Supplies _____   Account #: _21348871-0411_

Amount: _Four hundred and------------ .00/100_   Dollars   $ _____ 400.00 _____

Re: _____ Bank Loan payment (principal and interest) _____

Signed by: _Guy Smith_

---

## Adjustment Information:

---

### Blue Wave Fishing Supplies

**Memo**

2637 Highway 18 East, North Bay, Ontario P1B 7G8

Date:   July 31, 2012
From:   Adeline Vogelgesang

Re:   Store Supplies _____

I have calculated the total cost of the Store Supplies on Hand as being $471.
Calculations are in the supplies file. Please make the appropriate adjustment for July.

Signed owner's name:   _Adeline_

---

### Blue Wave Fishing Supplies

**Memo**

2637 Highway 18 East, North Bay, Ontario P1B 7G8

Date:   July 31, 2012
From   Adeline Vogelgesang

Re:   Insurance _____

The Fire and Theft insurance policy remaining balance for July and August is $400.
Please make the appropriate adjustment for July. The Insurance file is located in my office.

Signed owner's name:   _Adeline_

---

## Blue Wave Fishing Supplies

2637 Highway 18 East, North Bay, Ontario P1B 7G8

# Memo

Date:     June 30, 2012  ( Copy of Original Memo )

To:       Adeline Vogelgesang, Owner

From:     Sarah Davis, Accounting Service

---

From information supplied by you.

Total value of Store Equipment purchased is per Store Equipment General Ledger Account #161.
All equipment was purchased on January 2, 2010.

Normal life expectancy for this type of equipment is 5 years.

Estimated trade-in allowance is approximately $ 1,500.00.

Based on the above, we have adjusted the amortization on a monthly basis to June 30. We would suggest you make a monthly entry to adjust amortization.

I have photocopied this memo, to remind you to process a monthly transaction.

*Sarah Davis*

## Blue Wave Fishing Supplies

2637 Highway 18 East, North Bay, Ontario P1B 7G8

# Memo

Date:     July 31, 2012
From:     Adeline Vogelgesang

Re:       Business Taxes

---

The $120.00 Business Tax Expense for July has not been accrued.
Please make the appropriate adjustment for July.
The Business Tax file is located in my office.

Signed owner's name:     *Adeline*

---

**List of Journal Forms Provided** (*SP* refers to **Special Journal** with Perpetual Inventory columns).

| *Title* | *Type of Transaction* | *Page No's* |
| --- | --- | --- |
| Special Journals | | |
| *SP* Sales Journal | for credit sales | S7 |
| *SP* Cash Receipts Journal | for cash received | CR6 |
| *SP* Purchase Journal | for credit purchases | P5 |
| *SP* Cash Disbursements Journal | for cash payments | CD8 |
| General Journal | for other transactions | GJ7 to GJ11 |

*Note*: Students recording transactions without using the Special Journals can record transactions in the General Journal, pages 35 to 39.

**List of Additional Accounting Forms Provided**

General Ledger Accounts with balances

Subledger accounts – Accounts Receivable with balances

Subledger accounts – Accounts Payable with balances

Subledger accounts – Inventory items with amounts

Blank Worksheet for July

Blank form for Income Statement

Blank form for Statement of Changes in Owner's Equity

Blank form for Balance Sheet

Blank form for Subledger Ledger Balances

Blank form for Inventory items

Blank form for Ratio calculations

# Special Journals Decision Tree

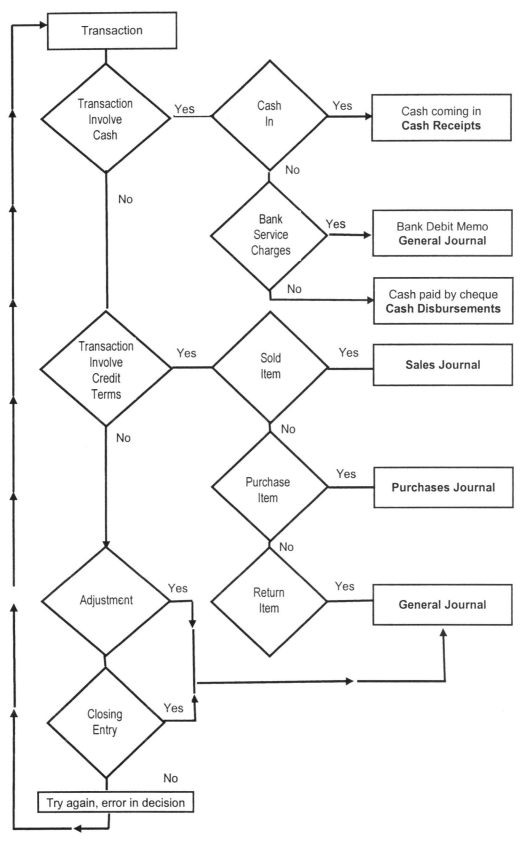

# SPECIAL JOURNALS

# SALES JOURNAL *with Perpetual Inventory*

| Date | Name Of Customer | Inv. No. | Terms | Accounts Receivable | Post Ref. | Sales Rod Reels | Sales Tackle Boxes | Sales Nets | Sales Other | GST on Sales | PST Payable | Cost of Goods Sold | Mdse Inventory | Inven Post Ref * |
|------|------------------|----------|-------|---------------------|-----------|-----------------|--------------------|------------|-------------|--------------|-------------|--------------------|----------------|------------------|
|  |  |  |  |  |  |  |  |  |  |  |  |  |  |  |
|  |  |  |  |  |  |  |  |  |  |  |  |  |  |  |
|  |  |  |  |  |  |  |  |  |  |  |  |  |  |  |
|  |  |  |  |  |  |  |  |  |  |  |  |  |  |  |
|  |  |  |  |  |  |  |  |  |  |  |  |  |  |  |
|  |  |  |  |  |  |  |  |  |  |  |  |  |  |  |
|  |  |  |  |  |  |  |  |  |  |  |  |  |  |  |

\* You will use a ✓ to indicate that you have posted the inventory values to the inventory subledger.

# CASH RECEIPTS JOURNAL *with Perpetual Inventory*

| Date | Name Of Customer | Inv./ Cheque No. | Cash | Sales Disct. | Accounts Receivable | Post Ref. | Sales Rod Reel | Sales Tackle Boxes | Sales Nets | Sales Other | GST on Sales | PST Payable | Cost of Goods Sold | Mdse Inven-tory | Inven Post Ref * |
|------|------------------|------------------|------|--------------|---------------------|-----------|----------------|--------------------|------------|-------------|--------------|-------------|--------------------|------------------|------------------|
|  |  |  |  |  |  |  |  |  |  |  |  |  |  |  |  |
|  |  |  |  |  |  |  |  |  |  |  |  |  |  |  |  |
|  |  |  |  |  |  |  |  |  |  |  |  |  |  |  |  |
|  |  |  |  |  |  |  |  |  |  |  |  |  |  |  |  |
|  |  |  |  |  |  |  |  |  |  |  |  |  |  |  |  |
|  |  |  |  |  |  |  |  |  |  |  |  |  |  |  |  |
|  |  |  |  |  |  |  |  |  |  |  |  |  |  |  |  |
|  |  |  |  |  |  |  |  |  |  |  |  |  |  |  |  |

\* You will use a ✓ to indicate that you have posted the inventory values to the inventory subledger.

## PURCHASE JOURNAL *with Perpetual Inventory*

| Date | Name Of Supplier | Inv. No. | Terms | Accounts Payable | Sub Post Ref. | Merchandise Inventory | Inven Post Ref.* | Store Supplies On Hand | GST on Purc/Serv | Other Acct. Name | Post Ref. | Other Amount |
|------|------------------|----------|-------|------------------|---------------|----------------------|------------------|------------------------|------------------|------------------|-----------|--------------|
|  |  |  |  |  |  |  |  |  |  |  |  |  |
|  |  |  |  |  |  |  |  |  |  |  |  |  |
|  |  |  |  |  |  |  |  |  |  |  |  |  |
|  |  |  |  |  |  |  |  |  |  |  |  |  |

\* You will use a ✓ to indicate that you have posted the inventory values to the inventory subledger.

## CASH DISBURSEMENTS JOURNAL

| Date | Cheque Issued To | Inv. No. Paid | Cheque Number | Cash | Purch. Discts. | Accounts Payable | Post Ref | GST On Purc/Serv | Other Account Names | Post Ref. | Other Amount |
|------|------------------|---------------|---------------|------|----------------|------------------|----------|------------------|---------------------|-----------|--------------|
|  |  |  |  |  |  |  |  |  |  |  |  |
|  |  |  |  |  |  |  |  |  |  |  |  |
|  |  |  |  |  |  |  |  |  |  |  |  |
|  |  |  |  |  |  |  |  |  |  |  |  |
|  |  |  |  |  |  |  |  |  |  |  |  |
|  |  |  |  |  |  |  |  |  |  |  |  |
|  |  |  |  |  |  |  |  |  |  |  |  |
|  |  |  |  |  |  |  |  |  |  |  |  |

| Date | Account Titles and Explanation | Post Ref. | Inven Post Ref. | Debit | | Credit | | Journal Used |
|---|---|---|---|---|---|---|---|---|
| | | | | | | | | |
| | | | | | | | | |
| | | | | | | | | |
| | | | | | | | | |
| | | | | | | | | |
| | | | | | | | | |
| | | | | | | | | |
| | | | | | | | | |
| | | | | | | | | |
| | | | | | | | | |
| | | | | | | | | |
| | | | | | | | | |
| | | | | | | | | |
| | | | | | | | | |
| | | | | | | | | |
| | | | | | | | | |
| | | | | | | | | |
| | | | | | | | | |
| | | | | | | | | |
| | | | | | | | | |
| | | | | | | | | |
| | | | | | | | | |
| | | | | | | | | |
| | | | | | | | | |
| | | | | | | | | |
| | | | | | | | | |
| | | | | | | | | |
| | | | | | | | | |
| | | | | | | | | |
| | | | | | | | | |
| | | | | | | | | |
| | | | | | | | | |
| | | | | | | | | |
| | | | | | | | | |
| | | | | | | | | |
| | | | | | | | | |
| | | | | | | | | |
| | | | | | | | | |
| | | | | | | | | |
| | | | | | | | | |
| | | | | | | | | |
| | | | | | | | | |
| | | | | | | | | |
| | | | | | | | | |
| | | | | | | | | |
| | | | | | | | | |
| | | | | | | | | |

| Date | Account Titles and Explanation | Post Ref. | Inven Post Ref. | Debit | | | Credit | | | Journal Used |
|---|---|---|---|---|---|---|---|---|---|---|
| | | | | | | | | | | |
| | | | | | | | | | | |
| | | | | | | | | | | |
| | | | | | | | | | | |
| | | | | | | | | | | |
| | | | | | | | | | | |
| | | | | | | | | | | |
| | | | | | | | | | | |
| | | | | | | | | | | |
| | | | | | | | | | | |
| | | | | | | | | | | |
| | | | | | | | | | | |
| | | | | | | | | | | |
| | | | | | | | | | | |
| | | | | | | | | | | |
| | | | | | | | | | | |
| | | | | | | | | | | |
| | | | | | | | | | | |
| | | | | | | | | | | |
| | | | | | | | | | | |
| | | | | | | | | | | |
| | | | | | | | | | | |
| | | | | | | | | | | |
| | | | | | | | | | | |
| | | | | | | | | | | |
| | | | | | | | | | | |
| | | | | | | | | | | |
| | | | | | | | | | | |
| | | | | | | | | | | |
| | | | | | | | | | | |
| | | | | | | | | | | |
| | | | | | | | | | | |
| | | | | | | | | | | |
| | | | | | | | | | | |
| | | | | | | | | | | |
| | | | | | | | | | | |
| | | | | | | | | | | |
| | | | | | | | | | | |
| | | | | | | | | | | |
| | | | | | | | | | | |
| | | | | | | | | | | |
| | | | | | | | | | | |
| | | | | | | | | | | |
| | | | | | | | | | | |

| Date | Account Titles and Explanation | Post Ref. | Inven Post Ref. | Debit | | | Credit | | | Journal Used |
|---|---|---|---|---|---|---|---|---|---|---|
| | | | | | | | | | | |
| | | | | | | | | | | |
| | | | | | | | | | | |
| | | | | | | | | | | |
| | | | | | | | | | | |
| | | | | | | | | | | |
| | | | | | | | | | | |
| | | | | | | | | | | |
| | | | | | | | | | | |
| | | | | | | | | | | |
| | | | | | | | | | | |
| | | | | | | | | | | |
| | | | | | | | | | | |
| | | | | | | | | | | |
| | | | | | | | | | | |
| | | | | | | | | | | |
| | | | | | | | | | | |
| | | | | | | | | | | |
| | | | | | | | | | | |
| | | | | | | | | | | |
| | | | | | | | | | | |
| | | | | | | | | | | |
| | | | | | | | | | | |
| | | | | | | | | | | |
| | | | | | | | | | | |
| | | | | | | | | | | |
| | | | | | | | | | | |
| | | | | | | | | | | |
| | | | | | | | | | | |
| | | | | | | | | | | |
| | | | | | | | | | | |
| | | | | | | | | | | |
| | | | | | | | | | | |
| | | | | | | | | | | |
| | | | | | | | | | | |

| Date | Account Titles and Explanation | Post Ref. | Inven Post Ref. | Debit | | Credit | | Journal Used |
|---|---|---|---|---|---|---|---|---|
| | | | | | | | | |
| | | | | | | | | |
| | | | | | | | | |
| | | | | | | | | |
| | | | | | | | | |
| | | | | | | | | |
| | | | | | | | | |
| | | | | | | | | |
| | | | | | | | | |
| | | | | | | | | |
| | | | | | | | | |
| | | | | | | | | |
| | | | | | | | | |
| | | | | | | | | |
| | | | | | | | | |
| | | | | | | | | |
| | | | | | | | | |
| | | | | | | | | |
| | | | | | | | | |
| | | | | | | | | |
| | | | | | | | | |
| | | | | | | | | |
| | | | | | | | | |
| | | | | | | | | |
| | | | | | | | | |
| | | | | | | | | |
| | | | | | | | | |
| | | | | | | | | |
| | | | | | | | | |
| | | | | | | | | |
| | | | | | | | | |
| | | | | | | | | |
| | | | | | | | | |
| | | | | | | | | |
| | | | | | | | | |
| | | | | | | | | |
| | | | | | | | | |
| | | | | | | | | |
| | | | | | | | | |
| | | | | | | | | |
| | | | | | | | | |
| | | | | | | | | |

| Date | Account Titles and Explanation | Post Ref. | Inven Post Ref. | Debit | | | Credit | | | Journal Used |
|------|-------------------------------|-----------|------------------|-------|---|---|--------|---|---|--------------|
| | | | | | | | | | | |
| | | | | | | | | | | |
| | | | | | | | | | | |
| | | | | | | | | | | |
| | | | | | | | | | | |
| | | | | | | | | | | |
| | | | | | | | | | | |
| | | | | | | | | | | |
| | | | | | | | | | | |
| | | | | | | | | | | |
| | | | | | | | | | | |
| | | | | | | | | | | |
| | | | | | | | | | | |
| | | | | | | | | | | |
| | | | | | | | | | | |
| | | | | | | | | | | |
| | | | | | | | | | | |
| | | | | | | | | | | |
| | | | | | | | | | | |
| | | | | | | | | | | |
| | | | | | | | | | | |
| | | | | | | | | | | |
| | | | | | | | | | | |
| | | | | | | | | | | |
| | | | | | | | | | | |
| | | | | | | | | | | |
| | | | | | | | | | | |
| | | | | | | | | | | |
| | | | | | | | | | | |
| | | | | | | | | | | |
| | | | | | | | | | | |
| | | | | | | | | | | |
| | | | | | | | | | | |
| | | | | | | | | | | |
| | | | | | | | | | | |
| | | | | | | | | | | |
| | | | | | | | | | | |
| | | | | | | | | | | |
| | | | | | | | | | | |
| | | | | | | | | | | |
| | | | | | | | | | | |
| | | | | | | | | | | |
| | | | | | | | | | | |
| | | | | | | | | | | |
| | | | | | | | | | | |

# Chart of General Ledger Accounts – Perpetual *Inventory*

| Account Number | Account Name |
|------|------------------------------------------|
| ------ | ----------------------------------------- |
| 101 | Bank Account Chequing |
| 120 | Accounts Receivable |
| 122 | Merchandise Inventory |
| 124 | Store Supplies on Hand |
| 128 | Prepaid Insurance |
| 161 | Store Equipment |
| 162 | Accumulated Amortization Store Equipment |
| 210 | Accounts Payable |
| 220 | Business Taxes Payable |
| 241 | GST on Sales |
| 243 | GST on Purc/Serv |
| 248 | PST Payable |
| 261 | Bank Loan Payable  (Long-Term) |
| 310 | Capital    A. Vogelgesang |
| 315 | Drawings A. Vogelgesang |
| 401 | Sales – Rod & Reel sets |
| 403 | Sales – Tackle Boxes |
| 405 | Sales – Nets |
| 407 | Sales – Other |
| 421 | Sales – Returns |
| 423 | Sales – Discounts |
| 510 | Cost of Goods Sold |
| 516 | Purchase Discounts |
| 521 | Rent Expense |
| 523 | Store Salaries Expense |
| 525 | Security Expense |
| 527 | Store Supplies Expense |
| 529 | Insurance Expense |
| 531 | Hydro and Water Expense |
| 533 | Amortization Expense Equipment |
| 535 | Advertising Expenses |
| 537 | Business Taxes Expense |
| 572 | Miscellaneous Expense |
| 574 | Bank Charges/Interest Expense |
| 576 | Bookkeeping Expense |

## SUBLEDGERS

| | | |
|---|---|---|
| Accounts receivable subledger | (customer numbers | C1-C5) |
| Accounts payable subledger | (supplier numbers | S1-S5) |
| Inventory items subledger | (various item numbers) | |

ACCOUNT **Bank Account Chequing** NO. **101**

| DATE | | EXPLANATION | PR | DEBIT | | | CREDIT | | | BALANCE | | | DR |
|---|---|---|---|---|---|---|---|---|---|---|---|---|---|
| June | 30 | Balance Forward | / | | | | | | | 15 | 625 | - | DR |
| | | | | | | | | | | | | | |
| | | | | | | | | | | | | | |
| | | | | | | | | | | | | | |
| | | | | | | | | | | | | | |
| | | | | | | | | | | | | | |
| | | | | | | | | | | | | | |
| | | | | | | | | | | | | | |
| | | | | | | | | | | | | | |
| | | | | | | | | | | | | | |
| | | | | | | | | | | | | | |
| | | | | | | | | | | | | | |
| | | | | | | | | | | | | | |
| | | | | | | | | | | | | | |
| | | | | | | | | | | | | | |

ACCOUNT **Accounts Receivable** NO. **120**

| DATE | | EXPLANATION | PR | DEBIT | | | CREDIT | | | BALANCE | | | DR |
|---|---|---|---|---|---|---|---|---|---|---|---|---|---|
| June | 30 | Balance Forward | / | | | | | | | 3 | 210 | - | DR |
| | | | | | | | | | | | | | |
| | | | | | | | | | | | | | |
| | | | | | | | | | | | | | |
| | | | | | | | | | | | | | |
| | | | | | | | | | | | | | |
| | | | | | | | | | | | | | |
| | | | | | | | | | | | | | |
| | | | | | | | | | | | | | |
| | | | | | | | | | | | | | |
| | | | | | | | | | | | | | |
| | | | | | | | | | | | | | |

ACCOUNT **Merchandise Inventory** NO. **122**

| DATE | | EXPLANATION | PR | DEBIT | | | CREDIT | | | BALANCE | | | DR |
|---|---|---|---|---|---|---|---|---|---|---|---|---|---|
| June | 30 | Balance Forward | / | | | | | | | 5 | 150 | - | DR |
| | | | | | | | | | | | | | |
| | | | | | | | | | | | | | |
| | | | | | | | | | | | | | |
| | | | | | | | | | | | | | |
| | | | | | | | | | | | | | |
| | | | | | | | | | | | | | |
| | | | | | | | | | | | | | |
| | | | | | | | | | | | | | |
| | | | | | | | | | | | | | |
| | | | | | | | | | | | | | |

ACCOUNT  **Store Supplies on Hand**                                          NO. **124**

| DATE | | EXPLANATION | PR | DEBIT | | | CREDIT | | | BALANCE | | DR CR |
|---|---|---|---|---|---|---|---|---|---|---|---|---|
| June | 30 | Balance Forward | / | | | | | | | 378 | - | DR |
| | | | | | | | | | | | | |
| | | | | | | | | | | | | |
| | | | | | | | | | | | | |

ACCOUNT  **Prepaid Insurance**                                          NO. **128**

| DATE | | EXPLANATION | PR | DEBIT | | | CREDIT | | | BALANCE | | DR CR |
|---|---|---|---|---|---|---|---|---|---|---|---|---|
| June | 30 | Balance Forward | / | | | | | | | 400 | - | DR |
| | | | | | | | | | | | | |
| | | | | | | | | | | | | |

ACCOUNT  **Store Equipment**                                          NO. **161**

| DATE | | EXPLANATION | PR | DEBIT | | | CREDIT | | | BALANCE | | DR CR |
|---|---|---|---|---|---|---|---|---|---|---|---|---|
| June | 30 | Balance Forward | / | | | | | | 31 | 500 | - | DR |
| | | | | | | | | | | | | |

ACCOUNT  **Accumulated Amortization Store Equipment**                                          NO. **162**

| DATE | | EXPLANATION | PR | DEBIT | | | CREDIT | | | BALANCE | | DR CR |
|---|---|---|---|---|---|---|---|---|---|---|---|---|
| June | 30 | Balance Forward | / | | | | | | 15 | 000 | - | CR |
| | | | | | | | | | | | | |
| | | | | | | | | | | | | |

ACCOUNT  **Accounts Payable**                                          NO. **210**

| DATE | | EXPLANATION | PR | DEBIT | | | CREDIT | | | BALANCE | | DR CR |
|---|---|---|---|---|---|---|---|---|---|---|---|---|
| June | 30 | Balance Forward | / | | | | | | 3 | 103 | - | CR |
| | | | | | | | | | | | | |
| | | | | | | | | | | | | |
| | | | | | | | | | | | | |
| | | | | | | | | | | | | |
| | | | | | | | | | | | | |
| | | | | | | | | | | | | |

# GENERAL LEDGER – *Perpetual Inventory*

ACCOUNT  **Business Taxes Payable**                                          NO. **220**

| DATE | | EXPLANATION | PR | DEBIT | CREDIT | BALANCE | DR CR |
|---|---|---|---|---|---|---|---|
| June | 30 | Balance Forward | / | | | -0- | CR |
| | | | | | | | |
| | | | | | | | |

ACCOUNT  **GST on Sales**                                          NO. **241**

| DATE | | EXPLANATION | PR | DEBIT | CREDIT | BALANCE | DR CR |
|---|---|---|---|---|---|---|---|
| June | 30 | Balance Forward | / | | | 1 501 - | CR |
| | | | | | | | |
| | | | | | | | |
| | | | | | | | |
| | | | | | | | |
| | | | | | | | |
| | | | | | | | |
| | | | | | | | |
| | | | | | | | |

ACCOUNT  **GST on Purc/Serv**                                          NO. **243**

| DATE | | EXPLANATION | PR | DEBIT | CREDIT | BALANCE | DR CR |
|---|---|---|---|---|---|---|---|
| June | 30 | Balance Forward | / | | | 786 - | DR |
| | | | | | | | |
| | | | | | | | |
| | | | | | | | |
| | | | | | | | |
| | | | | | | | |
| | | | | | | | |
| | | | | | | | |
| | | | | | | | |

ACCOUNT  **PST Payable**                                          NO. **248**

| DATE | | EXPLANATION | PR | DEBIT | CREDIT | BALANCE | DR CR |
|---|---|---|---|---|---|---|---|
| June | 30 | Balance Forward | / | | | 40 - | CR |
| | | | | | | | |
| | | | | | | | |
| | | | | | | | |

ACCOUNT  **Bank Loan Payable (Long-Term)**  NO. **261**

| DATE | | EXPLANATION | PR | DEBIT | CREDIT | BALANCE | DR CR |
|---|---|---|---|---|---|---|---|
| June | 30 | Balance Forward | / | | | 10 072 - | CR |
| | | | | | | | |
| | | | | | | | |

ACCOUNT  **Capital A. Vogelgesang**  NO. **310**

| DATE | | EXPLANATION | PR | DEBIT | CREDIT | BALANCE | DR CR |
|---|---|---|---|---|---|---|---|
| June | 30 | Balance Forward | / | | | 8 325 - | CR |
| | | | | | | | |

ACCOUNT  **Drawings A. Vogelgesang**  NO. **315**

| DATE | | EXPLANATION | PR | DEBIT | CREDIT | BALANCE | DR CR |
|---|---|---|---|---|---|---|---|
| June | 30 | Balance Forward | / | | | 3 600 - | DR |
| | | | | | | | |
| | | | | | | | |

ACCOUNT  **Sales — Rod & Reel sets**  NO. **401**

| DATE | | EXPLANATION | PR | DEBIT | CREDIT | BALANCE | DR CR |
|---|---|---|---|---|---|---|---|
| June | 30 | Balance Forward | / | | | 59 256 - | CR |
| | | | | | | | |
| | | | | | | | |
| | | | | | | | |
| | | | | | | | |
| | | | | | | | |

ACCOUNT  **Sales — Tackle Boxes**  NO. **403**

| DATE | | EXPLANATION | PR | DEBIT | CREDIT | BALANCE | DR CR |
|---|---|---|---|---|---|---|---|
| June | 30 | Balance Forward | / | | | 43 200 - | CR |
| | | | | | | | |
| | | | | | | | |
| | | | | | | | |
| | | | | | | | |

ACCOUNT   **Sales — Nets**                                                          NO. **405**

| DATE | | EXPLANATION | PR | DEBIT | | CREDIT | | BALANCE | | DR CR |
|---|---|---|---|---|---|---|---|---|---|---|
| June | 30 | Balance Forward | / | | | | | 19 | 780 - | CR |
| | | | | | | | | | | |
| | | | | | | | | | | |
| | | | | | | | | | | |

ACCOUNT   **Sales — Other**                                                          NO. **407**

| DATE | | EXPLANATION | PR | DEBIT | | CREDIT | | BALANCE | | DR CR |
|---|---|---|---|---|---|---|---|---|---|---|
| June | 30 | Balance Forward | / | | | | | 6 | 400 - | CR |
| | | | | | | | | | | |
| | | | | | | | | | | |
| | | | | | | | | | | |
| | | | | | | | | | | |
| | | | | | | | | | | |

ACCOUNT   **Sales — Returns**                                                          NO. **421**

| DATE | | EXPLANATION | PR | DEBIT | | CREDIT | | BALANCE | | DR CR |
|---|---|---|---|---|---|---|---|---|---|---|
| June | 30 | Balance Forward | / | | | | | | 830 - | DR |
| | | | | | | | | | | |
| | | | | | | | | | | |

ACCOUNT   **Sales — Discounts**                                                          NO. **423**

| DATE | | EXPLANATION | PR | DEBIT | | CREDIT | | BALANCE | | DR CR |
|---|---|---|---|---|---|---|---|---|---|---|
| June | 30 | Balance Forward | / | | | | | 2 | 124 - | DR |
| | | | | | | | | | | |
| | | | | | | | | | | |

ACCOUNT   **Cost of Goods Sold**                                                          NO. **510**

| DATE | | EXPLANATION | PR | DEBIT | | CREDIT | | BALANCE | | DR CR |
|---|---|---|---|---|---|---|---|---|---|---|
| June | 30 | Balance Forward | / | | | | | 64 | 634 - | DR |
| | | | | | | | | | | |
| | | | | | | | | | | |
| | | | | | | | | | | |
| | | | | | | | | | | |
| | | | | | | | | | | |
| | | | | | | | | | | |

ACCOUNT **Purchase Discounts**                                    NO. **516**

| DATE | | EXPLANATION | PR | DEBIT | | | CREDIT | | | BALANCE | | | DR CR |
|---|---|---|---|---|---|---|---|---|---|---|---|---|---|
| June | 30 | Balance Forward | / | | | | | | | 1 | 195 | - | CR |
| | | | | | | | | | | | | | |
| | | | | | | | | | | | | | |

ACCOUNT **Rent Expense**                                          NO. **521**

| DATE | | EXPLANATION | PR | DEBIT | | | CREDIT | | | BALANCE | | | DR CR |
|---|---|---|---|---|---|---|---|---|---|---|---|---|---|
| June | 30 | Balance Forward | / | | | | | | | 12 | 000 | - | DR |
| | | | | | | | | | | | | | |
| | | | | | | | | | | | | | |

ACCOUNT **Store Salaries Expense**                               NO. **523**

| DATE | | EXPLANATION | PR | DEBIT | | | CREDIT | | | BALANCE | | | DR CR |
|---|---|---|---|---|---|---|---|---|---|---|---|---|---|
| June | 30 | Balance Forward | / | | | | | | | 12 | 650 | - | DR |
| | | | | | | | | | | | | | |
| | | | | | | | | | | | | | |

ACCOUNT **Security Expense**                                      NO. **525**

| DATE | | EXPLANATION | PR | DEBIT | | | CREDIT | | | BALANCE | | | DR CR |
|---|---|---|---|---|---|---|---|---|---|---|---|---|---|
| June | 30 | Balance Forward | / | | | | | | | | 600 | - | DR |
| | | | | | | | | | | | | | |
| | | | | | | | | | | | | | |

ACCOUNT **Store Supplies Expense**                               NO. **527**

| DATE | | EXPLANATION | PR | DEBIT | | | CREDIT | | | BALANCE | | | DR CR |
|---|---|---|---|---|---|---|---|---|---|---|---|---|---|
| June | 30 | Balance Forward | / | | | | | | | | 941 | - | DR |
| | | | | | | | | | | | | | |
| | | | | | | | | | | | | | |

ACCOUNT **Insurance Expense**                                     NO. **529**

| DATE | | EXPLANATION | PR | DEBIT | | | CREDIT | | | BALANCE | | | DR CR |
|---|---|---|---|---|---|---|---|---|---|---|---|---|---|
| June | 30 | Balance Forward | / | | | | | | | 1 | 200 | - | DR |
| | | | | | | | | | | | | | |
| | | | | | | | | | | | | | |

ACCOUNT **Hydro and Water Expense** NO. **531**

| DATE | | EXPLANATION | PR | DEBIT | | | CREDIT | | | BALANCE | | DR CR |
|---|---|---|---|---|---|---|---|---|---|---|---|---|
| June | 30 | Balance Forward | / | | | | | | | 512 | - | DR |
| | | | | | | | | | | | | |
| | | | | | | | | | | | | |

ACCOUNT **Amortization Expense Equipment** NO. **533**

| DATE | | EXPLANATION | PR | DEBIT | | | CREDIT | | | BALANCE | | DR CR |
|---|---|---|---|---|---|---|---|---|---|---|---|---|
| June | 30 | Balance Forward | / | | | | | | | 3 000 | - | DR |
| | | | | | | | | | | | | |
| | | | | | | | | | | | | |

ACCOUNT **Advertising Expenses** NO. **535**

| DATE | | EXPLANATION | PR | DEBIT | | | CREDIT | | | BALANCE | | DR CR |
|---|---|---|---|---|---|---|---|---|---|---|---|---|
| June | 30 | Balance Forward | / | | | | | | | 6 680 | - | DR |
| | | | | | | | | | | | | |
| | | | | | | | | | | | | |

ACCOUNT **Business Taxes Expense** NO. **537**

| DATE | | EXPLANATION | PR | DEBIT | | | CREDIT | | | BALANCE | | DR CR |
|---|---|---|---|---|---|---|---|---|---|---|---|---|
| June | 30 | Balance Forward | / | | | | | | | 720 | - | DR |
| | | | | | | | | | | | | |
| | | | | | | | | | | | | |

ACCOUNT **Miscellaneous Expense** NO. **572**

| DATE | | EXPLANATION | PR | DEBIT | | | CREDIT | | | BALANCE | | DR CR |
|---|---|---|---|---|---|---|---|---|---|---|---|---|
| June | 30 | Balance Forward | / | | | | | | | 260 | - | DR |
| | | | | | | | | | | | | |
| | | | | | | | | | | | | |

ACCOUNT **Bank Charges/Interest Expense** NO. **574**

| DATE | | EXPLANATION | PR | DEBIT | | | CREDIT | | | BALANCE | | DR CR |
|---|---|---|---|---|---|---|---|---|---|---|---|---|
| June | 30 | Balance Forward | / | | | | | | | 472 | - | DR |
| | | | | | | | | | | | | |
| | | | | | | | | | | | | |

ACCOUNT **Bookkeeping Expense** NO. **576**

| DATE | | EXPLANATION | PR | DEBIT | | | CREDIT | | | BALANCE | | DR CR |
|---|---|---|---|---|---|---|---|---|---|---|---|---|
| June | 30 | Balance Forward | / | | | | | | | 600 | - | DR |
| | | | | | | | | | | | | |
| | | | | | | | | | | | | |

# ACCOUNTS RECEIVABLE – CUSTOMERS

**Central Lake RV Centre**                                    ACCOUNT NO. **C1**

| DATE | EXPLANATION | PR | DEBIT | CREDIT | BALANCE | DR CR |
|------|-------------|----|-------|--------|---------|-------|
| June 01 | Balance Forward #680 | / | | | 1 070 - | DR |
| | | | | | | |
| | | | | | | |

**North River Lodge**                                          ACCOUNT NO. **C2**

| DATE | EXPLANATION | PR | DEBIT | CREDIT | BALANCE | DR CR |
|------|-------------|----|-------|--------|---------|-------|
| June 28 | Balance Forward #703 | / | | | 963 - | DR |
| | | | | | | |
| | | | | | | |

**Trout Lake Resort**                                          ACCOUNT NO. **C3**

| DATE | EXPLANATION | PR | DEBIT | CREDIT | BALANCE | DR CR |
|------|-------------|----|-------|--------|---------|-------|
| June 22 | Balance Forward #698 | / | | | 1 177 - | DR |
| | | | | | | |
| | | | | | | |
| | | | | | | |
| | | | | | | |

ACCOUNT NO. **C4**

| DATE | EXPLANATION | PR | DEBIT | CREDIT | BALANCE | DR CR |
|------|-------------|----|-------|--------|---------|-------|
| | Balance Forward | / | | | | DR |
| | | | | | | |
| | | | | | | |
| | | | | | | |
| | | | | | | |

ACCOUNT NO. **C5**

| DATE | EXPLANATION | PR | DEBIT | CREDIT | BALANCE | DR CR |
|------|-------------|----|-------|--------|---------|-------|
| | Balance Forward | / | | | | DR |
| | | | | | | |
| | | | | | | |
| | | | | | | |

# ACCOUNTS PAYABLE – SUPPLIERS

### Fishing Accessories Inc.

ACCOUNT NO. **S1**

| DATE | EXPLANATION | PR | DEBIT | CREDIT | BALANCE | DR CR |
|---|---|---|---|---|---|---|
| June 29 | Balance Forward #685 | / | | | 963 - | CR |
| | | | | | | |
| | | | | | | |
| | | | | | | |
| | | | | | | |

### Rods & Reels Company

ACCOUNT NO. **S2**

| DATE | EXPLANATION | PR | DEBIT | CREDIT | BALANCE | DR CR |
|---|---|---|---|---|---|---|
| June 29 | Balance Forward #2987 | / | | | 1 391 - | CR |
| | | | | | | |

### Laredo Tackle Boxes Ltd.

ACCOUNT NO. **S3**

| DATE | EXPLANATION | PR | DEBIT | CREDIT | BALANCE | DR CR |
|---|---|---|---|---|---|---|
| June 29 | Balance Forward #832 | / | | | 749 - | CR |
| | | | | | | |
| | | | | | | |
| | | | | | | |

ACCOUNT NO. **S4**

| DATE | EXPLANATION | PR | DEBIT | CREDIT | BALANCE | DR CR |
|---|---|---|---|---|---|---|
| | Balance Forward | / | | | | CR |
| | | | | | | |
| | | | | | | |

ACCOUNT NO. **S5**

| DATE | EXPLANATION | PR | DEBIT | CREDIT | BALANCE | DR CR |
|---|---|---|---|---|---|---|
| | Balance Forward | / | | | | CR |
| | | | | | | |
| | | | | | | |

# Perpetual Inventory Subledger

Note: The "Post Ref" column is used for the journal reference.
The Inventory Balance column "Unit Cost" is calculated to 4 decimal places.
The Sales "Unit Cost" is calculated from the Inventory Balance 'Unit Cost' to 4 decimal places.

Inventory Code: **CL-Lg**     Coolers- Large
Selling Price     $40.00

| Date | Post Ref | Units | Unit Cost | Total Cost | Units | Unit Cost 4 Decimals | Cost of Goods Sold | Units | Unit Cost 4 Decimals | Cost Inventory on hand |
|------|----------|-------|-----------|------------|-------|----------------------|--------------------|-------|----------------------|------------------------|
| | | **Purchases** | | | **Sales** | | | **Inventory Balance** | | |
| Jun 30 | | | | | | | | 6 | 20.0000 | 120.00 |
| | | | | | | | | | | |
| | | | | | | | | | | |
| | | | | | | | | | | |
| | | | | | | | | | | |

Inventory Code: **CL-Md**     Coolers- Medium
Selling Price     $30.00

| Date | Post Ref | Units | Unit Cost | Total Cost | Units | Unit Cost 4 Decimals | Cost of Goods Sold | Units | Unit Cost 4 Decimals | Cost Inventory on hand |
|------|----------|-------|-----------|------------|-------|----------------------|--------------------|-------|----------------------|------------------------|
| | | **Purchases** | | | **Sales** | | | **Inventory Balance** | | |
| Jun 30 | | | | | | | | 3 | 15.0000 | 45.00 |
| | | | | | | | | | | |
| | | | | | | | | | | |

Inventory Code:
Selling Price

| Date | Post Ref | Units | Unit Cost | Total Cost | Units | Unit Cost 4 Decimals | Cost of Goods Sold | Units | Unit Cost 4 Decimals | Cost Inventory on hand |
|------|----------|-------|-----------|------------|-------|----------------------|--------------------|-------|----------------------|------------------------|
| | | **Purchases** | | | **Sales** | | | **Inventory Balance** | | |
| Jun 30 | | | | | | | | | | 0.00 |
| | | | | | | | | | | |
| | | | | | | | | | | |
| | | | | | | | | | | |
| | | | | | | | | | | |

Inventory Code: **FH-1**     Assorted Fish Hooks
Selling Price     $10.00

| Date | Post Ref | Units | Unit Cost | Total Cost | Units | Unit Cost 4 Decimals | Cost of Goods Sold | Units | Unit Cost 4 Decimals | Cost Inventory on hand |
|------|----------|-------|-----------|------------|-------|----------------------|--------------------|-------|----------------------|------------------------|
| | | **Purchases** | | | **Sales** | | | **Inventory Balance** | | |
| Jun 30 | | | | | | | | 140 | 5.0000 | 700.00 |
| | | | | | | | | | | |
| | | | | | | | | | | |

# Perpetual Inventory Subledger

Inventory Code: **FL-1**      Fishing Line

Selling Price      $20.00

| Date | Post Ref | Purchases Units | Purchases Unit Cost | Purchases Total Cost | Sales Units | Sales Unit Cost 4 Decimals | Sales Cost of Goods Sold | Inventory Balance Units | Inventory Balance Unit Cost 4 Decimals | Inventory Balance Cost Inventory on hand |
|------|----------|-----------------|---------------------|----------------------|-------------|----------------------------|--------------------------|-------------------------|----------------------------------------|------------------------------------------|
| Jun 30 | | | | | | | | 33 | 10.0000 | 330.00 |
| | | | | | | | | | | |
| | | | | | | | | | | |

Inventory Code: **Net-Bes**      Net- Best

Selling Price      $70.00

| Date | Post Ref | Purchases Units | Purchases Unit Cost | Purchases Total Cost | Sales Units | Sales Unit Cost 4 Decimals | Sales Cost of Goods Sold | Inventory Balance Units | Inventory Balance Unit Cost 4 Decimals | Inventory Balance Cost Inventory on hand |
|------|----------|-----------------|---------------------|----------------------|-------------|----------------------------|--------------------------|-------------------------|----------------------------------------|------------------------------------------|
| Jun 30 | | | | | | | | 14 | 35.0000 | 490.00 |
| | | | | | | | | | | |
| | | | | | | | | | | |
| | | | | | | | | | | |

Inventory Code: **Net-Bet**      Net- Better

Selling Price      $50.00

| Date | Post Ref | Purchases Units | Purchases Unit Cost | Purchases Total Cost | Sales Units | Sales Unit Cost 4 Decimals | Sales Cost of Goods Sold | Inventory Balance Units | Inventory Balance Unit Cost 4 Decimals | Inventory Balance Cost Inventory on hand |
|------|----------|-----------------|---------------------|----------------------|-------------|----------------------------|--------------------------|-------------------------|----------------------------------------|------------------------------------------|
| Jun 30 | | | | | | | | 10 | 25.0000 | 250.00 |
| | | | | | | | | | | |
| | | | | | | | | | | |
| | | | | | | | | | | |

Inventory Code: **Rod-1**      Rod & Reel set - 1

Selling Price      $90.00

| Date | Post Ref | Purchases Units | Purchases Unit Cost | Purchases Total Cost | Sales Units | Sales Unit Cost 4 Decimals | Sales Cost of Goods Sold | Inventory Balance Units | Inventory Balance Unit Cost 4 Decimals | Inventory Balance Cost Inventory on hand |
|------|----------|-----------------|---------------------|----------------------|-------------|----------------------------|--------------------------|-------------------------|----------------------------------------|------------------------------------------|
| Jun 30 | | | | | | | | 12 | 45.0000 | 540.00 |
| | | | | | | | | | | |
| | | | | | | | | | | |

# Perpetual Inventory Subledger

Inventory Code: **Rod-2**  Rod & Reel set -2

Selling Price  $110.00

| Date | Post Ref | Purchases | | | Sales | | | Inventory Balance | | |
|---|---|---|---|---|---|---|---|---|---|---|
| | | Units | Unit Cost | Total Cost | Units | Unit Cost 4 Decimals | Cost of Goods Sold | Units | Unit Cost 4 Decimals | Cost Inventory on hand |
| Jun 30 | | | | | | | | 15 | 55.0000 | 825.00 |
| | | | | | | | | | | |
| | | | | | | | | | | |
| | | | | | | | | | | |
| | | | | | | | | | | |

Inventory Code: **Rod-3**  Rod Reel set - 3

Selling Price  $140.00

| Date | Post Ref | Purchases | | | Sales | | | Inventory Balance | | |
|---|---|---|---|---|---|---|---|---|---|---|
| | | Units | Unit Cost | Total Cost | Units | Unit Cost 4 Decimals | Cost of Goods Sold | Units | Unit Cost 4 Decimals | Cost Inventory on hand |
| Jun 30 | | | | | | | | 12 | 70.0000 | 840.00 |
| | | | | | | | | | | |
| | | | | | | | | | | |

Inventory Code: **TK-Bes**  Tackle Box- Best

Selling Price  $70.00

| Date | Post Ref | Purchases | | | Sales | | | Inventory Balance | | |
|---|---|---|---|---|---|---|---|---|---|---|
| | | Units | Unit Cost | Total Cost | Units | Unit Cost 4 Decimals | Cost of Goods Sold | Units | Unit Cost 4 Decimals | Cost Inventory on hand |
| Jun 30 | | | | | | | | 16 | 35.0000 | 560.00 |
| | | | | | | | | | | |
| | | | | | | | | | | |
| | | | | | | | | | | |
| | | | | | | | | | | |
| | | | | | | | | | | |

Inventory Code: **TK-Bet**  Tackle Box- Better

Selling Price  $50.00

| Date | Post Ref | Purchases | | | Sales | | | Inventory Balance | | |
|---|---|---|---|---|---|---|---|---|---|---|
| | | Units | Unit Cost | Total Cost | Units | Unit Cost 4 Decimals | Cost of Goods Sold | Units | Unit Cost 4 Decimals | Cost Inventory on hand |
| Jun 30 | | | | | | | | 18 | 25.0000 | 450.00 |
| | | | | | | | | | | |
| | | | | | | | | | | |
| | | | | | | | | | | |
| | | | | | | | | | | |
| | | | | | | | | | | |

Blue Wave Fishing Supplies
Worksheet
For 7 months ending July 31, 2012

You can download the Excel Spreadsheet "WsJuly-Perpetual.xls" from www.freedman.nelson.com to complete the worksheet.

| | | ACCOUNT TITLES | Trial Balance | | Adjustments | | Adjusted Trial Balance | | Income Statement | | Balance Sheet | |
|---|---|---|---|---|---|---|---|---|---|---|---|---|
| | | | Debit | Credit | Debit | Credit | Debit | Credit | Debit | Credit | Debit | Credit |
| 101 | | Bank Account Chequing | | | | | | | | | | |
| 120 | | Accounts Receivable | | | | | | | | | | |
| 122 | | Merchandise Inventory | | | | | | | | | | |
| 124 | | Store Supplies on Hand | | | | | | | | | | |
| 128 | | Prepaid Insurance | | | | | | | | | | |
| 161 | | Store Equipment | | | | | | | | | | |
| 162 | | Accum Amortiz Store Equip | | | | | | | | | | |
| 210 | | Accounts Payable | | | | | | | | | | |
| 220 | | Business Taxes Payable | | | | | | | | | | |
| 241 | | GST on Sales | | | | | | | | | | |
| 243 | | GST on Purc/Serv | | | | | | | | | | |
| 248 | | PST Payable | | | | | | | | | | |
| 261 | | Bank Loan Payable | | | | | | | | | | |
| 310 | | Capital A. Vogelgesang | | | | | | | | | | |
| 315 | | Drawings A. Vogelgesang | | | | | | | | | | |
| 401 | | Sales - Rod & Reel sets | | | | | | | | | | |
| 403 | | Sales - Tackle Boxes | | | | | | | | | | |
| 405 | | Sales - Nets | | | | | | | | | | |
| 407 | | Sales - Other | | | | | | | | | | |
| 421 | | Sales - Returns | | | | | | | | | | |
| 423 | | Sales - Discounts | | | | | | | | | | |
| 510 | | Cost of Goods Sold | | | | | | | | | | |
| 516 | | Purchase - Discounts | | | | | | | | | | |
| 521 | | Rent Expense | | | | | | | | | | |
| 523 | | Store Salaries Expense | | | | | | | | | | |
| 525 | | Security Expense | | | | | | | | | | |
| 527 | | Store Supplies Expense | | | | | | | | | | |
| 529 | | Insurance Expense | | | | | | | | | | |
| 531 | | Hydro and Water Expense | | | | | | | | | | |
| 533 | | Amortization Exp Equip | | | | | | | | | | |
| 535 | | Advertising Expenses | | | | | | | | | | |
| 537 | | Business Taxes Expense | | | | | | | | | | |
| 572 | | Miscellaneous Expense | | | | | | | | | | |
| 574 | | Bank Charges/Interest Expense | | | | | | | | | | |
| 576 | | Bookkeeping Expense | | | | | | | | | | |
| | | | | | | | | | | | | |
| | | Net Income for period | | | | | | | | | | |

**An Accounting Practice Set**

**Blue Wave Fishing Supplies**
**Income Statement**
**For**

**Blue Wave Fishing Supplies**
**Statement of Changes in Owner's Equity**
**For**

|  |  |  |  |  |  |  |
|---|---|---|---|---|---|---|
|  |  |  |  |  |  |  |
|  |  |  |  |  |  |  |
|  |  |  |  |  |  |  |
|  |  |  |  |  |  |  |
|  |  |  |  |  |  |  |
|  |  |  |  |  |  |  |
|  |  |  |  |  |  |  |
|  |  |  |  |  |  |  |
|  |  |  |  |  |  |  |

**Blue Wave Fishing Supplies**
**Balance Sheet**
**For**

**Blue Wave Fishing Supplies**

**Blue Wave Fishing Supplies**
**Schedule of Accounts Receivable**
**For**

| | | | | | | | |
|---|---|---|---|---|---|---|---|
| | | | | | | | |
| | | | | | | | |
| | | | | | | | |
| | | | | | | | |
| | | | | | | | |
| | | | | | | | |
| | | | | | | | |
| | | | | | | | |

**Blue Wave Fishing Supplies**
**Schedule of Accounts Payable**
**For**

| | | | | | | | |
|---|---|---|---|---|---|---|---|
| | | | | | | | |
| | | | | | | | |
| | | | | | | | |
| | | | | | | | |
| | | | | | | | |
| | | | | | | | |
| | | | | | | | |
| | | | | | | | |

**Blue Wave Fishing Supplies**
**Schedule of Inventory items**
**For**

| | Units | Weighted Average Cost | | Total Cost | |
|---|---|---|---|---|---|
| CL-Lg  Coolers- Large | | | | | |
| CL-Md Coolers- Medium | | | | | |
| | | | | | |
| FH-1 Assorted Fish hooks | | | | | |
| FL-1 Fishing line | | | | | |
| Net-Bes  Net Best | | | | | |
| Net-Bet   Net Better | | | | | |
| Rod-1 Rod Reel set 1 | | | | | |
| Rod-1 Rod Reel set 2 | | | | | |
| Rod-1 Rod Reel set 3 | | | | | |
| TK-Bes Tackle Box- Best | | | | | |
| TK-Bet Tackle Box- Better | | | | | |
| | | | | | |
| | | | | | |

**An Accounting Practice Set**

Blue Wave Fishing Supplies
Ratio Analysis
For

**Current Ratio**

$\dfrac{\text{Current Assets}}{\text{Current Liabilities}} =$

**Acid Test Ratio**

$\dfrac{\text{Quick Assets}}{\text{Current Liabilities}} =$

**Gross Profit Ratio**

$\dfrac{\text{Gross Profit from Sales}}{\text{Net Sales}} =$

**Expense Ratio**

$\dfrac{\text{Operating Expenses}}{\text{Net Sales}} =$

**Net Profit Ratio**

$\dfrac{\text{Net Profit}}{\text{Net Sales}} =$

**Merchandise Turnover**

$\dfrac{\text{Cost of Goods Sold}}{\text{Average Cost of Inventory}} =$

**Return on Equity**

$\dfrac{\text{Net Income (Profit)}}{\text{Beginning Owner's Equity}} =$

**Debt Ratio**

$\dfrac{\text{Total Liabilities}}{\text{Total Assets}} =$

## Additional Questions

The financial data is now complete. The following are general business questions an owner would need to know about their business. What advice would you give Mrs. Vogelgesang now that you have had time to review the information?

1.      Is the business going very well?

2.      Mrs. Vogelgesang is managing her inventory purchases well. (Why or why not?)

3.      Mrs. Vogelgesang has been asked by a few customers to stock fillet knives (special knives for cleaning fish). She has a chance to buy a selection of these knives (individual cost prices from $7.00 to $15.00) with a minimum investment of $1,000.00. Should she buy the knives?

4.      After the close of business on July 31, the Credit Bureau reported that the "Noble's Teen Camp" is classified as a 1A business. This means that they have a good credit rating. Should Mrs. Vogelgesang offer to change their recent order to 2/10, n30 days and give them a discount on the partial payment?

5.      Based on the ratio analysis, what are two ratios that are causing Mrs. Vogelgesang to reconsider previous decisions and why?

6.      What changes should be made to the business in order to make sure the business succeeds in the future?

7.      Are there any bill(s) or invoices that were not paid or accrued?

**Simply Accounting® by Sage, Income Statement**

**Blue Wave Fishing Supplies**
**Income Statement Jan 01, 2012 to Jun 30, 2012**

**REVENUE**

| | | |
|---|---|---|
| Sales - Rod & Reel sets | 59,256.00 | |
| Sales - Tackle Boxes | 43,200.00 | |
| Sales - Nets | 19,780.00 | |
| Sales - Other | 6,400.00 | |
| Total Sales | | 128,636.00 |
| Sales - Returns | -830.00 | |
| Sales - Discounts | -2,124.00 | |
| Total Deductions | | -2,954.00 |
| **Net Sales** | | 125,682.00 |
| | | |
| **TOTAL REVENUE** | | 125,682.00 |

**EXPENSE**

**Cost of Goods Sold**

| | |
|---|---|
| Cost of Goods Sold | 64,634.00 |
| Purchase- Discounts | -1,195.00 |
| **Net Cost of Goods Sold** | 63,439.00 |

**Sales Expenses**

| | |
|---|---|
| Rent Expense | 12,000.00 |
| Store Salaries Expense | 12,650.00 |
| Security Expense | 600.00 |
| Store Supplies Expense | 941.00 |
| Insurance Expense | 1,200.00 |
| Hydro and Water Expense | 512.00 |
| Amortization Expense Store | 3,000.00 |
| Advertising Expense | 6,680.00 |
| Business Taxes Expenses | 720.00 |
| **Total Sales Expense** | 38,303.00 |

**General Expenses**

| | |
|---|---|
| Miscellaneous Expense | 260.00 |
| Bank Charges/Interest Expense | 472.00 |
| Bookkeeping Expense | 600.00 |
| **Total General Expenses** | 1,332.00 |

| | |
|---|---|
| **TOTAL EXPENSE** | 39,635.00 |
| | |
| **NET INCOME** | 22,608.00 |

## Bank Reconciliation Form

You may complete the Bank Reconciliation below. The Bank Statement is on the next page.

Blue Wave Fishing Supplies
Bank Reconciliation
As

Balance per Bank     $                       Balance per Books     $

Add:                                            Add:

Subtotal        _____     Subtotal        _____

Less:                                         Less:

Reconciled Balance   $ _____     Reconciled Balance   $ _____

The following statement from the North Bay Bank was received on August 9, 2012.
Prepare a Bank Reconciliation as of July 31, 2012 in proper form.

The Bank Reconciliation Adjustments have not been included in the solution but may be determined and included at the discretion of the instructor.

North Bay Bank
309 Massey Drive
North Bay, Ontario
P1A 9B6

Blue Wave Fishing Supplies
2637 Highway 18 East
North Bay, Ontario
P1B 7G8

Account Number: 21348871-0411

Statement period 1 Jul 2012 to 31 Jul 2012
Enclosed items 8                                                Page 1

| Date | | Ch.No. Or code | Withdrawals | Deposits | Balance |
|------|------|------|------|------|------|
| July | 1 | | | | 15,625.00 |
| | 2 | 612 | 2,140.00 | | 13,485.00 |
| | 4 | 613 | 107.00 | | 13,378.00 |
| | 9 | 614 | 1,365.00 | | 12,013.00 |
| | 18 | 615 | 642.00 | | 11,371.00 |
| | 20 | Dep | | 500.00 | 11,871.00 |
| | 20 | Dep | | 2,013.00 | 13,884.00 |
| | 23 | Dep | | 151.00 | 14,035.00 |
| | 24 | Cor | 151.00 | | 13,884.00 |
| | 26 | Dep | | 115.00 | 13,999.00 |
| | 24 | 616 | 642.00 | | 13,357.00 |
| | 31 | DB | 400.00 | | 12,957.00 |
| | 31 | 617 | 1,040.00 | | 11,917.00 |
| | 31 | DD | | 14.50 | 11,931.50 |
| | 31 | S/C | 9.00 | | 11,922.50 |
| | 31 | NSF | 115.00 | | 11,807.50 |

| | |
|------|------|
| DB | Debit Memo |
| DD | Direct Deposit |
| NSF | Not Sufficient Funds, Item returned |
| ACI | Item returned Account Closed |
| S/C | Service Charge |
| Cor | Correction |

The $14.50 deposit on July 31 was a direct deposit of Mrs. Vogelgesang personal GST rebate that should have been deposited into her personal chequing account. The Bank will make the transfer to her personal account. Mrs.Vogelgesang is sending a letter to Canada Revenue Agency to correct the error in banking information.

The NSF item is the returned friend's cheque from invoice #715. The friend has been contacted and is bringing in a certified cheque or cash to cover the NSF cheque.

## GST – Goods and Services Tax and Provincial Sales Tax

### Goods and Services Tax (GST)

The Goods and Services Tax (GST), presently at 7%, is levied by the Federal Government of Canada on most Goods and Services sold in Canada. Everyone, including businesses, must pay GST on their purchase. However, to avoid double taxation, a business is allowed to deduct the GST paid on its purchases from the GST it collects from its sales.

The business will either send the difference (more GST collected than paid) or will claim a refund (more paid than collected) to the Receiver General for Canada. Depending on the size of the business, it will report on a monthly or quarterly basis.

### Harmonized Sales Tax

New Brunswick, Nova Scotia, and Newfoundland and Labrador have adopted the Harmonized Sales Tax (HST) which is 15%. The HST works similar to the GST.

### Provincial Sales Tax (PST)

Provinces (except Alberta) levy (PST) provincial sales taxes and may include or exclude the GST in the price on which the PST is calculated. Blue Wave Fishing Supplies **does not include** the GST in calculating the PST.

### Registration for GST

A business with annual sales of more than $30,000 **must** register to collect the GST. Registering will allow a business to recover any GST paid on their purchases. Registration is optional for a business where sales will be less than $30,000.

**Blue Wave Fishing Supplies** uses the "**Regular Method**" of managing the GST. The business will record GST, collected on each sale and paid on goods and services purchased from suppliers. At the end of the reporting period the firm will deduct the GST paid from the GST collected and file for a refund or send the balance owing to the Receiver General for Canada.

## The Moving Average (Weighted) Cost of Inventory Method

The moving average cost of the merchandise inventory remaining in inventory (not sold) is recalculated each time a purchase is made.

**Feb 1**   60 Teddy Bears are purchased for sale at $10 to be sold at $20.00.

Inventory Code: **TB-01**      Teddy Bear- Gold

Selling Price      $20.00

| Date | Post Ref | Purchases | | | Sales | | | Inventory Balance | | |
|------|----------|-----------|-----------|------------|-------|---------------------|---------------------|-------|---------------------|------------------------|
| | | Units | Unit Cost | Total Cost | Units | Unit Cost 4 Decimals | Cost of Goods Sold | Units | Unit Cost 4 Decimals | Cost Inventory on hand |
| Feb 1 | | 60 | 10.00 | 600.00 | | | | 60 | 10.0000 | 600.00 |
| | | | | | | | | | | |

**Feb 3**   40 Teddy Bears are sold at $20.00, but the inventory record is shown at the recorded average cost ($10.00).

Inventory Code: **TB-01**      Teddy Bear- Gold

Selling Price      $20.00

| Date | Post Ref | Purchases | | | Sales | | | Inventory Balance | | |
|------|----------|-----------|-----------|------------|-------|---------------------|---------------------|-------|---------------------|------------------------|
| | | Units | Unit Cost | Total Cost | Units | Unit Cost 4 Decimals | Cost of Goods Sold | Units | Unit Cost 4 Decimals | Cost Inventory on hand |
| Feb 1 | | 60 | 10.00 | 600.00 | | | | 60 | 10.0000 | 600.00 |
| Feb 3 | | | | | 40 | 10.0000 | 400.00 | 20 | 10.0000 | 200.00 |
| | | | | | | | | | | |

**Feb 4**   50 more Teddy Bears are purchased at a higher price $12.00 and the average cost increases. Note: As the price of new purchases goes higher, the average cost rises.

There are now 20 bears at a cost of $10.000 each and 50 bears at a cost of $12.00 each. There are now 70 bears at a combined cost of $800.00.

$$\begin{array}{lll} 20 & \text{at } 10 = & \$200.00 \\ \underline{50} & \text{at } 12 = & \underline{\$600.00} \\ 70 & & \$800.00 \end{array}$$

Inventory Code: **TB-01**      Teddy Bear- Gold

Selling Price      $20.00

| Date | Post Ref | Purchases | | | Sales | | | Inventory Balance | | |
|------|----------|-----------|-----------|------------|-------|---------------------|---------------------|-------|---------------------|------------------------|
| | | Units | Unit Cost | Total Cost | Units | Unit Cost 4 Decimals | Cost of Goods Sold | Units | Unit Cost 4 Decimals | Cost Inventory on hand |
| Feb 1 | | 60 | 10.00 | 600.00 | | | | 50 | 10.0000 | 600.00 |
| Feb 3 | | | | | 40 | 10.00 | 400.00 | 20 | 10.0000 | 200.00 |
| Feb 4 | | 50 | 12.00 | 600.00 | | | | 70 | 11.4286 | 800.00 |
| | | | | | | | | | | |

The new average cost of the 70 bears increases to: 11.42857171
$800.00 / 70 bears is 11.42857171
Most computer software records the average inventory cost to 4 decimal places for accuracy.
New average is       11.4286

**Feb 5**   The next sale of 30 Teddy Bears at cost is now at $11.4286 each.

Inventory Code: **TB-01**     Teddy Bear- Gold
Selling Price     $20.00

| Date | Post Ref | Purchases | | | Sales | | | Inventory Balance | | |
|---|---|---|---|---|---|---|---|---|---|---|
| | | Units | Unit Cost | Total Cost | Units | Unit Cost 4 Decimals | Cost of Goods Sold | Units | Unit Cost 4 Decimals | Cost Inventory on hand |
| Feb 1 | | 60 | 10.00 | 600.00 | | | | 60 | 10.0000 | 600.00 |
| Feb 3 | | | | | 40 | 10.0000 | 400.00 | 20 | 10.0000 | 200.00 |
| Feb 4 | | 50 | 12.00 | 600.00 | | | | 70 | 11.4286 | 800.00 |
| Feb 5 | | | | | 30 | 11.4286 | 342.86 | 40 | 11.4286 | 457.14 |
| | | | | | | | | | | |

**Feb 7**   20 more Teddy Bears are purchased at a higher price $12.00 and the average cost increases.

There are now 40 bears at a cost of $11.4286 each and 20 bears at a cost of $12.00 each.
There are now 60 bears at a combined cost of $697.14.

$$\begin{array}{rll} 40 \text{ at} & 11.4286 = & \$457.14 \\ \underline{20} \text{ at} & 12.0000 = & \underline{\$240.00} \\ 60 & & \$697.14 \end{array}$$

Inventory Code: **TB-01**     Teddy Bear- Gold
Selling Price     $20.00

| Date | Post Ref | Purchases | | | Sales | | | Inventory Balance | | |
|---|---|---|---|---|---|---|---|---|---|---|
| | | Units | Unit Cost | Total Cost | Units | Unit Cost 4 Decimals | Cost of Goods Sold | Units | Unit Cost 4 Decimals | Cost Inventory on hand |
| Feb 1 | | 60 | 10.00 | 600.00 | | | | 60 | 10.0000 | 600.00 |
| Feb 3 | | | | | 40 | 10.0000 | 400.00 | 20 | 10.0000 | 200.00 |
| Feb 4 | | 50 | 12.00 | 600.00 | | | | 70 | 11.4286 | 800.00 |
| Feb 5 | | | | | 30 | 11.4286 | 342.86 | 40 | 11.4286 | 457.14 |
| Feb 7 | | 20 | 12.00 | 240.00 | | | | 60 | 11.6190 | 697.14 |

The new average cost of the 60 bears increases to: 11.6190
        $697.14 / 60 bears is 11.6190

If the price of new purchases decreases, the average cost will decrease as well.